New Nutshells

Trusts
in a Nutshell

Other Titles in the Series

Company Law
Constitutional Law
Contract
Criminal Law
English Legal System
Employment Law
Family Law
International Trade
Jurisprudence
Land Law
Sale of Goods and Consumer Credit
Tort

AUSTRALIA
The Law Book Company Ltd.
Sydney : Melbourne : Brisbane

CANADA AND U.S.A.
The Carswell Company Ltd.
Agincourt, Ontario

INDIA
N.M. Tripathi Private Ltd.
Bombay
and
Eastern Law House Private Ltd.
Calcutta
M.P.P. House
Bangalore

ISRAEL
Steimatzky's Agency Ltd.
Jerusalem : Tel Aviv : Haifa

MALAYSIA : SINGAPORE : BRUNEI
Malayan Law Journal (Pte.) Ltd.
Singapore

NEW ZEALAND
Sweet and Maxwell (N.Z.) Ltd.
Auckland

PAKISTAN
Pakistan Law House
Karachi

New Nutshells

Trusts in a Nutshell

C. E. F. Rickett

London
Sweet & Maxwell
1980

Published in 1980 by
Sweet & Maxwell Ltd. of
11 New Fetter Lane, London.
Set by CET Graphics of Cheltenham, Glos.
Printed in Great Britain by
J. W. Arrowsmith Ltd.,
London and Bristol

Reprinted 1981

British Library Cataloguing in Publication Data

Rickett, C E F
  Trusts in a nutshell.—(New nutshells).
  1. Trusts and trustees-England
  I. Title II. Series
  346'.42'059   KD1480

ISBN 0-421-26540-X

Series Introduction

New Nutshells present the essential facts of law. Written in clear, uncomplicated language, they explain basic principles and highlight key cases and statutes.

New Nutshells meet a dual need for students of law or related disciplines. They provide a concise introduction to the central issues surrounding a subject, preparing the reader for detailed complementary textbooks. Then, they act as indispensable revision aids.

Produced in a convenient pocketbook format, *New Nutshells* serve both as invaluable guides to the most important questions of law and as reassuring props for the anxious examination candidate.

Trusts deals, first, with express trusts and looks at the various prerequisites which apply—certainty, that there be a human beneficiary, formalities and complete constitution. Separate chapters are then devoted to secret, implied and resulting, and constructive trusts.

Charity provides the concluding topic, with a review of definition, schemes and the doctrine of *cy-pres*.

Contents

	page
Series Introduction	v
Introduction	1
1 Express Trusts—The Prerequisite of Certainty	3
2 Express Trusts—The Prerequisite of a Human Beneficiary; and non-Charitable Purpose Trusts	10
3 Express Trusts—The Prerequisite of Formalities	21
4 Express Trusts—The Prerequisite of Complete Constitution; and Contracts to Create Trusts	29
5 Secret Trusts	44
6 Implied and Resulting Trusts	54
7 Constructive Trusts	65
8 Charity—Definition, Schemes and *Cy-pres*	75
Index	88

Introduction

The aim of this book is to pinpoint the core of the modern English law of trusts—its basic rules, principles and characteristics. It is hoped to provide a quick and easy, but, it must be stressed, *very simple*, guide for students in need of last minute revision notes. The really important work should already have been done; the textbooks, the articles and, above all, the central cases read. It is also hoped that others who wish to know a little about trusts will find something of use and interest in the book. There is, it must be said, almost nothing in the book on the administrative aspects of the law of trusts, that is the appointment and termination of appointment of trustees, the duties, disabilities and powers of trustees, and remedies for breach of trust. This is largely a result of lack of space, but also because these areas, in my experience, do not present the average student with the quality of challenge and interest which he generally finds in the areas actually dealt with in the book.

Some general points must be made. Historically, the trust is a creation of equity, that branch of legal rules and principles which evolved from the exercise of the extraordinary jurisdiction of the Chancellor in supplementing the rules of the common law wherever they were defective. The trust itself appears to have been a useful method of settling property, in particular land, so as to avoid liability for feudal dues and the operation of the mortmain statutes. Many modern trusts are established with tax avoidance or tax planning in mind, and revenue considerations are of immense practical importance in the day to day establishment and administration of trusts. This book does not touch on such points.

Outside fiscal considerations, express trusts today are created for a variety of reasons. Private family settlements are usually in the form of trusts, either very simple bare trusts or complex fixed or discretionary trusts. (It should be noted here that where land is held in trusts, it is usually under a strict settlement or trust for sale, as provided for in the 1925 property legislation—this area is covered in books on land law.) Clubs, societies, pension schemes, benevolent funds and charities often hold their property under trusts. Of growing importance are unit trusts, which provide an attractive means for the small investor of investment in a varied portfolio.

What is a trust? Essentially, description proves more satisfactory than definition in this area, but it is helpful to have before us at this stage the definition of Underhill, adopted with some modification by P. H. Pettit (*Equity and the Law of Trusts*, 4th ed., p. 17): "A trust is an equitable obligation, binding a person (who is called a trustee) to deal with property over which he has control (which is called the trust property) either for the benefit of persons (who are called the beneficiaries or *cestuis que trust*) of whom he may himself be one, and any one of whom may enforce the obligation, or for a charitable purpose, which may be enforced at the instance of the Attorney-General, or for some other purpose permitted by law though unenforceable." A trust gives rise to a "split ownership" in property. In essence, the trustee owns a title to the property, which title can be either legal or equitable, while the beneficiary owns the real or factual benefit of the property, which "ownership" is capable of vindication in equity. (*Baker* v. *Archer-Shee*, 1927; *Archer-Shee* v. *Garland*, 1931.) *Cf.* discretionary trusts, where the beneficiaries cannot "own" the property.

Trusts are usually classified and discussed in a threefold manner. An express trust arises where there is an expressed intention to set up the trust—this is the paradigm case of the substantive institution called the trust. An implied or resulting trust arises in three well-defined situations, to be discussed herein. A constructive trust arises when a trust is imposed by the court regardless of the intention of the owner of the property.

1 Express Trusts— The Prerequisite of Certainty

In *Knight* v. *Knight* (1840) Lord Langdale re-affirmed that for a trust to be valid the "three certainties" have to be satisfied.

1.*Certainty of words or intention*

Did the settlor or testator intend to set up a trust; as opposed perhaps to expressing a mere wish or desire, or imposing only a moral obligation? During the nineteenth century a fairly liberal approach was adopted, and precatory words in gifts would almost of themselves set up a trust. In *Re Adams and the Kensington Vestry* (1884) it was affirmed that "what we have to look at is the whole of the will which we have to construe" (*per* Cotton L.J.). The modern approach is one of construction of the words used in every case, with any other admissible evidence, to evince the true intention of the settlor/testator. If there is no adequate intention of a trust, the donee takes absolutely.

Re Williams (1897) C.A.

Property was left "absolutely in the fullest confidence that she will carry out my wishes in the following particulars. . . ." It was held by two to one that there was no trust, and the property belonged to the donee absolutely. Lindley L.J. said: ". . . (I)n each case the whole will must be looked at; and unless it appears from the whole will that an obligation was intended to be imposed, no obligation will be held to exist.

Re Kayford Ltd. (1975) Ch. Div.

A mail-order company took customers' moneys with their orders for the supply of goods. The moneys were placed in a separate account pending delivery of the goods. The company then went into liquidation. It was held that a trust existed over the moneys for the customers. The company had manifested a clear intention to set up a trust. Its consistent attitude had been that the moneys sent remained in the beneficial ownership of those who had sent them.

2. *Certainty of subject-matter*

The whole property subject to the trust must be certain. It must be capable of identification at the time the trust is intended to come into effect. If there is no clear trust property, there is nothing upon which the trust can fasten. In an alleged trust of "the bulk of my property" the transaction fails at the outset. It is probable also that there will not be a clear intention to establish a trust if there is no clear subject-matter. There can, of course, be a trust of "the residue of my estate."

Sprange v. Barnard (1789) Ch. Ct.

A testator left property for her husband's "sole use," but "at his death, the remaining part of what is left" was to be divided for others. There was no trust. It was not certain what would remain at his death. He thus took beneficially.

Cf. Re Last (1958) P.D.A. Div.

A testatrix left all her property to her brother, "(a)t his death anything that is left, that came from me to go to my

4

late husband's grandchildren. . . ." It was held that, looking at the will as a whole, and trying to give effect to the testator's clear wishes, the intention in legal terms was that the brother have a life interest. Thus the alleged trust would not fail for uncertainty of subject-matter. The trust existed over *all* the property, with different interests in the beneficiaries.

Often included under certainty of subject-matter is certainty of the actual beneficial interests to be taken by the beneficiaries. The whole trust property might be a number of houses. If the settlor fails to identify which of the houses is to go to which of the beneficiaries, the *express* trust fails. The usual result would be for the property to be held on resulting trust by the intended trustees for the settlor or his estate.

Boyce v. Boyce (1849) Ch. Ct.

A testator devised two houses to trustees on trust to convey to Maria whichever she chose, the other for Charlotte. Maria died before the testator, having made no choice. Charlotte had no interest. The houses were held on resulting trust.

It is a moot point whether in such a case the court would give effect to the general intention to benefit the identified beneficiaries, and divide the whole identified property equally (equity is equality), even though the particular intention failed. *Cf. Burrough* v. *Philcox* (1840).

There is no uncertainty in cases of discretionary trusts where the trustees must ascertain the quantum of the beneficial interests; nor in cases where an objective standard of assessment can be used by the court (see *Re Golay*, 1965—"reasonable income").

3. *Certainty of beneficiaries/objects*

This matter is often discussed in the context of the distinction between powers and trusts. Four juridical concepts must be distinguished—the fixed trust, the mere power of appointment, the fixed trust in default of appointment, and the pure discretionary trust.

A fixed trust is one where the quantum of the beneficial interests is fixed by the settlor, and hence *all* the beneficiaries must be ascertained. A gift in equal shares for "all my children" necessitates that the trustees know *all* the children so as to give them equal shares of the property. If no complete list can be drawn up, the expressed trust fails, and there is a resulting trust. See *contra* this view, D.B. Parker and A.R. Mellows, *The Modern Law of Trusts*, 4th Edit., at pp. 73-74.

We must now distinguish trusts from powers. A trust is imperative—it must ultimately be performed. This is very clear in cases of fixed trusts, where the beneficiaries "own" the property in a factual sense. Even where trustees have a discretion to determine which individuals among a class will benefit, and the extent to which they will benefit, the trust must ultimately be performed: *e.g.* "to such of my children and in such shares as my trustees see fit." A power on the other hand, is only discretionary—it may be performed in any way consistent with its terms, but it need not be performed. The question whether a particular provision is imperative or discretionary is one of construction. It arises most often in provisions for appointment of property among a limited class of persons. What looks like a mere power of appointment might be a trust power, or discretionary trust, and vice-versa. It may also be a mere power of appointment superimposed onto a fixed trust in equal shares—this often happens in family trust cases.

Burrough v. Philcox (1840) Ch. Ct.

A testator gave to his surviving child a power of appointment of his property to such of his nieces and nephews and their children, and in such shares, as the child should think proper. No appointment was ever made. As a matter of construction, the court held that there was a trust in favour of the nieces and nephews and their children in equal shares. It was a fixed trust (fixed really because the court would not undertake the exercise of any discretion, *cf. McPhail* v. *Doulton*, 1970; *Re Locker's Settlement Trusts*, 1978) to be implied in default of the exercise of the power of appointment. See also *Re Will's Trust Deeds* (1963).

This construction is rather odd, and is limited to the family trust cases. There are two important aspects. First, although categorised above as mere powers, in most cases these powers are referred to as *trust* powers. Thus the courts see themselves as stepping in to exercise imperative powers, and in doing so give effect to the "general intention" to benefit the specified family class by creating implied trusts. In other cases of *pure* discretionary trusts, even in cases before *McPhail* v. *Doulton* (see below), the courts could exercise the imperative powers of the trustees without recourse to an implied trust. It appears that although in *Burrough* v. *Philcox* the child held a trust power, he would not have been characterised as a discretionary trustee. Pettit has suggested that "trust power" be limited in use to this special case. Secondly, if there is a *fixed* trust in equal shares, it will only be valid if *all* the intended beneficiaries are ascertainable, which is usually so in family cases.

A power of appointment may be a trust power in the sense that the donee of the power *must* exercise it. He is a discretionary trustee, and there is a pure discretionary trust. Although beneficiaries under such a trust, unlike a fixed trust, do not "own" property, they will have a right against the donee of the power that the power be exercised. The court will thus step in to exercise the power if need be. It will take the place of the discretionary trustee, unlike in the case of a family trust where the court appears to ignore the power.

The nature of the courts' role in relation to mere powers—one of passivity, except in the case of an *ultra vires* exercise of the power— and that in relation to discretionary trusts—one of ever possible activity—led to a distinction in the tests of certainty applied to the specified class of beneficiaries to determine the validity of the power or trust. The test for discretionary trusts had to be stiffer, as the court would only act through equal division amongst *all* the beneficiaries. The class had to be so defined that all its members could be listed. Although the court was exercising the trust power of appointment, it would not take on a discretion peculiar to the named donee of the power. This reasoning is prominent in *I.R.C.* v. *Broadway Cottages Trust* (1955), and in statements of Lord Upjohn in *Re Gulbenkian's Settlement* (1970).

The test of certainty for mere powers was always more liberal, although not clearly defined until 1970.

Re Gulbenkian's Settlement (1970) H.L.

A clause in a settlement granted a special power of appointment exercisable for the maintenance and personal support for all or any one or more of a class—the husband, wife, children or remoter issue or any persons in whose house or appartments or in whose company or under whose care and control or by whom the husband might from time to time be employed or residing—as the trustee should in its absolute discretion think fit. The power was construed as a mere power and was held valid within the test. Lord Upjohn said that a mere power "is valid if you can with certainty say whether any given individual is or is not a member of the class; you do not have to ascertain every member of the class." Prediction must be possible for the court as regards *any* individual in the world, and not just one individual.

A further test related to certainty which appears to be applicable to mere powers is one of capriciousness, the negativing in the terms of the power of any sensible intention on the part of the donor of the power. See *Re Manisty's Settlement* (1974).

The test of certainty for discretionary trusts was assimilated to that for mere powers very soon after *Gulbenkian*.

McPhail v. Doulton (1970) H.L.

A deed provided for the making of grants out of the income of an invested fund in such amounts and to such of the staff of a company and their relatives and dependants as the trustees in their absolute discretion deemed fit. Their Lordships held this to be a trust, and by three to two held that the test of certainty for discretionary trusts is whether it can be said with certainty that any given individual is or is not a member of the class.

Re Baden's Deed Trust (No. 2) (1972) C.A.

The test had now to be applied to the clause in question. The Court of Appeal found difficulty in discovering what type of certainty was relevant and drew a distinction between conceptual or linguistic certainty (see Megaw and Sachs L.JJ.) and evidential certainty (see Stamp L.J.). It does, however, seem that both aspects of certainty must be attained. This is clear from the manner in which "relatives" was dealt with. Sachs and Megaw L.JJ. defined "relatives" as descendants of a common ancestor, and held this to be conceptually certain, since a substantial number of persons fell within the class. It would also be evidentially possible to determine whether any postulant was a relative. Further, if he could not prove he was a relative, then he must be not a relative. Stamp L.J. could not adopt this reasoning. He suggested that it must be possible to say of any postulant affirmatively that he *was or was not* a relative, and this could not be so of any descendants of a common ancestor. However, in defining "relatives" as next-of-kin, there would not be this evidential uncertainty, nor would that be conceptual uncertainty.

Clearly there are still problems to be resolved by the courts in the actual application of the new test.

There remains an important practical distinction between mere powers and discretionary trusts which makes it still necessary to decide on the issue of construction. In discretionary trusts, those exercising a discretion must do so more conscientiously (*e.g.* make a very comprehensive inquiry before choosing) than in the case of mere powers. This follows from the imperative nature of the power, and from the fact that the potential beneficiaries have a right to be considered as members of the specified class (although the right may be effective only for a substantial number rather than for all).

As discretionary trusts have been assimilated to mere powers as far as certainty is concerned, it may be that the *Re Manisty* capriciousness test operates in the area of discretionary trusts as well as for mere powers. It is suggested however, that this case should be read in conjunction with the statement of Lord Wilberforce in *McPhail* v. *Doulton* to the effect that in some cases, although the class of beneficiaries is conceptually (and probably evidentially) certain, it is nevertheless "so hopelessly wide as not to form anything like a class so that the trust is administratively unworkable." The example given of a gift to the "residents of Greater London" is indicative that the administratively unworkable test needs further judicial elaboration. It may be based on numerical considerations or general practical considerations such as expense, or indeed even on the capriciousness of the gift, as in *Manisty*. See, generally (1974) 38 Conv. 269 (L. McKay).

If the expressed trust fails to take effect because its objects are uncertain, within either of the tests examined for fixed and discretionary trusts, the property will be held on a resulting trust for the settlor or his estate.

2 Express Trusts—The Prerequisite of a Human Beneficiary; and non-Charitable Purpose Trusts

It is often said that a further aspect of the certainties requirements for validity is that there be a human beneficiary under the trust. It is in this area that we come across two further classificatory distinctions in the law of trusts.

The first distinction is that between *private trusts* (*i.e.* trusts generally for persons where the latter have defined equitable interests in the property; or, in the case of discretionary trusts, the right to have equitable interests defined by the holder of the discretion) and *public trusts* (*i.e.* charitable trusts, where the trusts are established to promote purposes, rather than to give defined equitable interests in property to persons, and which purposes must satisfy an element of public benefit). In this distinction, the human beneficiary requirement does not operate for public trusts; and it is a truism so far as private trusts are concerned.

The second distinction introduces a third type of trust, that expressed to be for a purpose or for non-human beneficiaries (*e.g.* especially individual animals), where the purpose is simply not public enough to warrant validation as a charitable trust (*cf.* a trust for the benefit of animals is general, which is charitable). This often called a *pure* or *private purpose trust.* The term favoured here is *non-charitable purpose trust*—this prevents a muddling of this trust into the general category of traditional *private trusts* for persons. It has been held in a series of cases that the human beneficiary requirement must be satisfied in *all* attempted trusts, except public trusts and a few anomalous cases of non-charitable purpose trusts. Thus *all* non-charitable purpose trusts, except the strictly defined anomalous cases, fail *at the outset* for lack of a human beneficiary.

The following categorisation must be kept in mind in the discussion following:

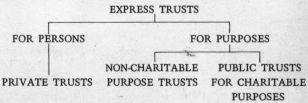

While valid *charitable* trusts remain linked to a concept of public benefit, there will always be attempts to establish non-charitable purpose trusts (see below at Chap. 8).

It is inevitable that a discussion of the human beneficiary principle should be a discussion of non-charitable purpose trusts. It is only here that it operates as a distinct requirement rather than as a truism.

1. *The rationale of the requirement*

In *Morice* v. *Bishop of Durham* (1805) Grant M.R. stated that "there must be somebody in whose favour the court can decree performance." Enforceability of the trustee's obligation to fulfil the terms of the trust is the essential point. A court cannot enforce or control a trust unless there exists an identified person interested under the trust who can bring any failure to perform or breach in performance to the notice of the court. In the case of charitable trusts, this position of initiation is occupied by the Attorney-General, and enforceability is satisfied.

A more general way of arguing the same point is to state simply that it is undesirable to permit a situation in which the execution of a trust depends solely upon the whim of a particular trustee, because he is not compellable.

Historically, there is much to be said for the general approach evidenced in the human beneficiary requirement. Equity has always acted *in personam*, fixing the conscience of the trustee with an obligation, intended to be enforceable through a legal process, to carry out the terms of the trust. But an obligation is fixed only when it is deemed that there should be a corresponding *right* in another person, and the latter has usually been identified as he who is intended by the settlor/testator to "own" the specified trust property in some beneficial manner (*cf. Re Denley's Trust Deed*, 1969). Thus, where there is no human beneficiary, there is no warrant for an obligation, no ground for a trust.

On the other hand, some criticisms can be levelled at the doctrine. First, it operates so as to invalidate, at least occasionally, trusts for purposes which appear prima facie to deserve support, certainly on a fairly liberal view. In *Re Shaw* (1957), for example, G.B. Shaw's attempt to provide funds for research into and the establishment of a new phonetic alphabet failed. It was not legally charitable, and there was no human beneficiary. Secondly, as a matter of principle and logic, there is a distinction between unenforceability and invalidity. It does not automatically follow that an obligation which cannot be enforced cannot therefore be a valid legal obligation, even in the face of contrary equity practice. Thirdly, it seems odd that questions of *human* beneficiaries should crop up in cases intended to cover purposes. The undesirable purpose cases can be weeded out by a test of capriciousness (*cf. Brown* v. *Burdett*, 1882) or a test of certainty which would invalidate "abstract or impersonal purposes" (see *Re Denley*, 1969, and *Re Astor's Settlement Trusts*, 1952). This may leave us, in practical terms, in precisely the situation we are in now, following *Re Denley* (see below). Nevertheless, it would be more satisfactory, in terms of principle, to jettison the human beneficiary requirement as the method of controlling the validity of non-charitable purpose gifts. Fourthly, if enforceability is seen as a fundamental prerequisite for validity, there seems no reason why *locus standi* for the purpose of enforceability should not be extended to persons not interested as direct (or even factual - following *Denley*) beneficiaries. In *Re Astor's Settlement Trusts* (1952), Roxburgh J. suggested that the so-called anomalous cases (to be discussed below) did not offend the need for enforceability, even if there were no human beneficiaries, since the trusts were controllable by the residuary beneficiaries or remaindermen. See, generally, (1973) 37 Conv. 420 (L. McKay). Carried to its ultimate bounds, this propostion is ridiculous. There are always residuary beneficiaries or remaindermen of some sort—in this sense then, the trust is always enforceable and always valid. But, secondly, those who would get the property in the event of the trust's failure seem to be the least suitable persons to turn to in order to ensure the trust's enforcement. If enforceability is to be taken this lightly, there is good reason to vest it in the settlor, or testator, or his estate, someone with a proper interest in enforcement. No purpose trust need fail for unenforceability.

2. *The scope of the requirement today*

In *Re Wood* (1949) Harman J. stated that "a gift on trust must have a *cestui que trust*." The need for a direct beneficiary, one who "owns" the property in a beneficial sense, was affirmed in *Re Astor* (1952) and *Re Endacott* (1960).

Leahy v. Attorney-General of New South Wales (1959) P.C.

A testator left his land, homestead and furniture "upon trust for such order of nuns of the Catholic Church or the Christian Brothers" as his executors should select. The gift was upheld under a New South Wales statute. However, it was further held that, without the statute, the gift would fail. It was a gift on trust, and even though the members of the selected order would benefit factually, this was not adequate to comply with the human beneficiary requirement.

Leahy was a decision basically about unincorporated associations. It is now out of date, and has been superceded by the modern approach (see below).

Re Denley's Trust Deed (1969) Ch. Div.

This case establishes the present scope of the human beneficiary requirement. Its general approach has been approved in *Re Lipinski's Will Trusts* (1976) (although this latter case itself presents difficulties). Trustees were directed to maintain and use some land as a sports ground for the benefit of the employees of a company, and any others they allowed in. Goff J. upheld the trust. The human beneficiary requirement only operates so as to invalidate purpose or object trusts which are abstract or impersonal, where the benefit to individuals is so indirect and intangible as not to give those persons any *locus standi* to apply to the court to enforce the trust. Where, however, the purpose is not too indirect or intangible, the human beneficiary requirement is satisfied by persons who have only a factual interest in the carrying out of the trust.

It is clear that private trusts for human beneficiaries must satisfy the certainty requirements outlined in Chapter 1. It is probable, however, that in cases of *Denley*-type non-charitable purpose trusts the prerequisite of certainty of objects must be satisfied in relation to the class of factual beneficiaries expressed (see Goff J. in *Denley*). This will probably be the *McPhail* v. *Doulton* discretionary trust test.

Furthermore, it is clear from *Re Astor* that all non-charitable purpose gifts which overcome the human beneficiary requirement (in whatever way) need to pass a more general test of certainty of purposes. Roxburgh J. held that the gift on trust for, *inter alia,* the establishment, maintenance and improvement of good understanding between nations, the preservation of the independance and integrity of newspapers, and the promotion of freedom of the press, failed not only for lack of a human beneficiary, but also for uncertainty. He said:

> "If . . . an enumeration of purposes outside the realm of charities can take the place of an enumeration of beneficiaries, the purposes must . . . be stated in phrases which embody definite concepts, and the means by which the trustees are to try to attain them must also be prescribed with a sufficient degree of certainty."

3. *The recognised exceptional cases*
Even after the liberal approach in *Re Denley,* some cases of gifts which would prima facie still fail under the new narrow version of the human beneficiary principle will nevertheless not fail because they are recognised as "concessions to human weakness or sentiment." As

indicated above, the exceptional cases *may* be restricted to trusts arising under wills, where, if the trust is not fulfilled, the legacy will fall into residue (see *Re Astor*). The cases are classified in five groupings:

(i) Trusts for the erection or maintenance of monuments or graves. See, for example, *Re Hooper* (1932) and *Pirbright* v. *Salwey* (1896). Cf. *Re Endacott* (1960) — gift "for the purpose of providing some useful memorial to myself" failed.

(ii) Trusts for the saying of masses. See *Re Caus* (1934); and *Carrigan* v. *Redwood* (1910) 30 N.Z.L.R. 244. Such trusts may be charitable (*cf. Gilmour* v. *Coates,* 1949).

(iii) Trusts for the maintenance or benefit of specific animals. See, for example, *Pettingall* v. *Pettingall* (1842), *Mitford* v. *Reynolds* (1848), *Re Dean* (1889), and *Re Haines* (1952).

It is interesting to note that in *Re Dean* North J. did not treat the case as an exceptional one at all. Indeed, he could *not* assent to the general proposition that "the court will not recognise a trust unless it is capable of being enforced by someone." It was only in *Re Astor* that *Re Dean* was treated as illustrating only a particular exception. It is, of course, possible that in the 19th Century the only cases of non-charitable purpose gifts to arise were those which now are classified as exceptions; and that had, say, *Re Endacott* or *Re Shaw*, or even *Re Astor*, come before North J., they might have been upheld. The human beneficiary principle might never have made an appearance.

(iv) Trusts for the benefit of unincorporated associations. This difficult area will be discussed below.

(v) The miscellaneous cases.

Re Thompson (1934) Ch. Div.

A testator left £1,000 to G.W.L. to be applied

16

at his discretion for the promotion and furtherance
of fox-hunting. Clauson J. upheld the trust, by
requiring G.W.L. to give an undertaking to apply
the legacy in the stipulated manner and by
granting the residuary legatees liberty to apply
to the court if G.W.L. failed to carry out the trust.

4. *The perpetuity question,*

A non-charitable purpose gift which overcomes the
first hurdle of the human beneficiary requirement has still
to jump another hurdle before it is valid. The purported
trust must not be capable of lasting in duration beyond a
relevant period of perpetuity.

Two points must be noted. First, the courts have
adopted a fairly liberal approach to this requirement. In
Mussett v. *Bingle* (1862) a gift for the *erection* of a
monument was upheld even though there was *no* mention
of any limitation of time in the gift; a gift for its
maintenance, without any limitation, however, failed. See
also *Re Budge* (1942) N.Z.L.R. 356. A trust will be upheld
if some phrase, even if very vague, is used indicating an
intention to limit legally its duration, e.g. "so long as the
law allows" (see *Re Hooper*). In this situation, the trust
will be upheld for a period of 21 years. On some occasions
judicial notice has been taken of the fact that an animal's
life span is under 21 years. Sometimes the assumption is
unwarranted (*e.g.* cats can live beyond 21 years; *cf. Re
Haines*). There has been criticism of the use of animals'
lives. If lives are to be used to measure the relevant period,
they should be human lives.

The second point relates to the particular period to be
used. There is strength in the argument that only a fixed
period, *e.g.* 21 years, should be allowed. No attention
should be paid to vague periods determined by lives, be
they human or animal. However, in *Re Astor* a royal lives
clause was not challenged; and in *Re Moore* (1901) the
argument was about the number of lives chosen rather than
about the very principle of lives. In *Re Khoo Cheng Teow*

(1932) the Supreme Court of the Straits Settlement upheld a non-charitable purpose trust for the period of royal lives plus 21 years. It is generally believed that the 80 year period introduced in the Perpetuities and Accumulations Act 1964 has no application whatever to purpose trusts; see section 15(4). Hanbury and Maudsley, *Modern Equity*, 10th ed., at pp. 360-361, presents an argument that the 80 year period may be used, under the statute, as an alternative to royal lives and 21 years.

5. *The problem of unincorporated associations*

   Unincorporated associations cannot legally hold or own property. However, on many occasions the very existence of the association indicates that something more is intended than simply an aggregate of the individual members; that the association exists for a particular purpose; and that any funds contributed by the members, or given by persons not members, are *intended* to be used for that purpose. Members who contribute generally intend to lose their sole beneficial ownership of the property contributed. Outside donors would usually be shocked if one supposed any other intention but to donate for the purposes, viewing the association perhaps as nothing more than an administrative mechanism. Much, of course, depends on the purpose of the association. Is it "inward-looking," *i.e.* interested in benefitting its members either directly or indirectly; or is it "outward-looking," *i.e.* interested in benefitting persons other than members, or in carrying out some impersonal purpose?

   If a gift is made to an unincorporated association for an expressed charitable purpose, or alternatively without more to an association which carries out charitable work, the gift will constitute a good charitable trust.

   If a gift is to an unincorporated non-charitable association, there appear to be four constructions available. (See *Re Recher's Will Trusts*, 1971).

   In some cases, particularly where the association exists to benefit the members themselves in some factual way, and there is in the rules no prohibition on the division or distribution of association property to the members, the gift may be construed as one to the individual members of the association at the date of the gift for their own benefit as joint tenants or tenants in common. This construction ensures the success of the gift.

A gift to the present and future members fails unless the duration of the gift is limited to the perpetuity period.

Thirdly, a gift may be held to be one to the trustees or officers of the association *on trust* to carry out the purposes of the association. This will be so if the terms of the gift show that it is made expressly on trust; or the rules governing the association indicate that members can have no beneficial interest in the property of the association. It used to be said that in this case the gift failed at the outset because it offended against the human beneficiary requirement. However, *Re Denley* has mitigated this effect, in that if the carrying out of the purpose will result in a factual benefit to ascertainable persons, the enforceability requirement is met. Strictly speaking, this case does not give rise to an exception to the beneficiary requirement; it is simply an area in which the beneficiary requirement is satisfied. Of course, a *Denley* construction will only succeed if the perpetuity condition is satisfied. In cases where the purposes of the association are abstract and impersonal, the gift will almost certainly fall foul of the human beneficiary requirement.

Fourthly, since *Neville Estates Ltd.* v. *Madden* (1961) and *Re Recher*, the basic construction has been that of the contract-holding theory. This avoids unfortunate questions of human beneficiaries and perpetuity. The basis is that the subject matter of the gift falls to be dealt with in accordance with the rules of the association by which the members are contractually bound *inter se*. No individual member can claim to be paid his share, although he is beneficially entitled, because this would be to breach his contract with the other members. If he dies or resigns, his share will accrue to the other members, including members

19

joining after the gift has taken effect. The contract-holding theory can also be used to construe the manner in which members' contributions are held. The property of the association, if held under this construction, will be distributable on dissolution among the members of the association at the time of dissolution. These basic principles were re-affirmed by Walton J. in *Re Bucks Constabulary Widows' and Orphans Fund Friendly Society (No. 2)* (1979). The contract-holding theory is not available when there is a clear expression of a trust imposed on the property, or, alternatively, the rules of the association forbid the retention of any beneficial interest by the members in the association's property.

Re Lipinski's Will Trusts (1976) Ch. Div.

Oliver J. dealt with this case as one of a gift to an unincorporated non-charitable association. First, he held there was no question of a gift to the members *individually*. He went on to uphold the gift as valid, apparently on two constructions. It was valid on the contract-holding theory. There was nothing in the rules of the society which prevented the members from vesting the property in themselves, and, supposedly, the terms of the gift were not inconsistent with such construction. Secondly, however, even if a *purpose trust* attached to the property, it would not fail for want of a human beneficiary, because the carrying out of the purpose would benefit ascertainable persons, the members (*Re Denley*). Further no question of perpetuity arose where the gift was an immediate gift of capital.

The case illustrates the use made of the various constructions, but it is unfortunate that the gift was upheld on *two* constructions, as each would lead logically to different results in the event of the association's dissolution. The destination of funds on dissolution is dependent on the correct interpretation of the manner in which they are held.

3 Express Trusts— The Prerequisite of Formalities

As a basic principle, it can be said that in connection with the creation of trusts, or dealings with equitable interests in property, there are no requirements relating to written formalities. This is so whether the transaction is *inter vivos* or testamentary; or whether the subject matter of the transaction is real or personal property. However, there are certain statutory requirements which are extremely important in practice. They cover a considerable number of cases.

1. *Contracts to create trusts; contracts to dispose of subsisting equitable interests*

   To be actionable, contracts relating to land or interests in land must comply with section 40(1) Law of Property Act 1925:

   > "No action may be brought upon any contract for the sale or other disposition of land or any interest in land, unless the agreement upon which such action is brought, or some memorandum or note thereof, is in writing, and signed by the party to be charged or by some other person thereunto by him lawfully authorised."

   The absence of writing as evidence of the contract does not make the contract void or illegal, but merely unenforceable by an action at law.

A contract relating to pure personality or any interest therein does not need to be in writing or evidenced by writing to be actionable.

It must be noted that a contract to assign an equitable interest in either land or personalty may be within section 53(1) (*c*) Law of Property Act 1925 as being a "disposition.. of a subsisting equitable interest (see discussion below of *Oughtred's case*).

2. Creation of trusts, and disposition of equitable interests by will

The Wills Act 1837 governs the testamentary disposition of all legal estates and equitable interests in both land and personalty. Section 9 reads:

> "No will shall be valid unless it shall be in writing . . . signed at the foot or end thereof by the testator, or by some other person in his presence and by his direction; and such signature shall be made or acknowledged by the testator in the presence of two or more witnesses present at the same time and such witnesses shall attest and shall subscribe the will in the presence of the testator, but no form of attestation shall be necessary."

Failure to comply with section 9 renders the will void.

3. Declarations of trust inter vivos

The law relating to formalities in this area is difficult, and a preliminary discussion is vital to an adequate under-standing. What is a "declaration of trust?" First, the owner of property can declare that henceforth he holds the property on trust—*declaration of self as trustee*. If he was absolute owner of the property, he will retain the legal title while the equitable interest will reside in the beneficiaries. If, however, he is declaring himself a trustee of an equitable interest he "owns," the resulting analysis depends on the nature of the newly declared trust, the sub-trust. A passive sub-trust arises where there is a bare, naked or simple trust,

22

i.e. where the trustee has no active duties to perform (and/or, questionably, where he holds as a trustee without any beneficial interest for himself). An active sub-trust, on the other hand, arises where the trustee does have active duties to perform. It is important to notice that an active sub-trust may be converted into a passive sub-trust on the performance by the trustee of his active duties. If the sub-trust is, or becomes, passive, it appears that the sub-trustee drops out and the legal owner becomes trustee for the ultimate beneficiary; see *Grainge* v. *Wilberforce* (1889) and *Re Lashmar* (1891). If the sub-trust is active, it becomes impossible for the sub-trustee to drop out. The sub-trustee therefore holds the equitable property as a trustee for the beneficiaries who have subsidiary equitable interests. Some statements in *Re Lashmar* appear to suggest that a sub-trustee holding property on successive interests without more is a passive sub-trustee and therefore drops out. This, it is suggested, is incorrect. A trustee holding on successive interests always has active duties to perform.

Secondly, the owner of property may create a trust by the transfer of that property to trustees, with a direction to the trustees to hold the property on specified trusts—*declaration of trust by transfer.*

Where a declaration of trust in land or any interest therein is intended, one must comply with section 53(1) (*b*) Law of Property Act 1925:

> "A declaration of trust respecting any land or any interest therein must be manifested and proved by some writing signed by some person who is able to declare such trust or by his will."

The writing is only required as evidence of the declaration, but must contain the material terms of the trust. The writing must be signed by the settlor. It is assumed that failure to comply with these evidential requirements will not make the trust void, but merely unenforceable. This is a strange situation, as it leaves a beneficial owner of

23

property with no protection. It is better to say that there is no trust at all, and that therefore no unenforceable beneficial interests are created.

Where a declaration of trust in pure personalty is intended, there is no requirement of form. Unsigned writing, word of mouth or even conduct is sufficient. See, for example, *Jones* v. *Lock* (1865).

Section 53(1) (*c*) Law of Property Act 1925 has caused some confusion. See, generally, (1979) Conv. 17 (G. Battersby). It reads:

> "A disposition of an equitable interest or trust subsisting at the time of the disposition, must be in writing signed by the person disposing of the same, or by his agent thereunto lawfully authorised in writing or by will."

As a result of judicial interpretation of the section it may be that some transactions which are prima facie *declarations of trust* over equitable interests within our definitions are also *dispositions* of subsisting equitable interests within section 53(1) (*c*).

Where a declaration of trust is a direction to the trustees by the equitable owner, at least where the equitable interest concerned is in pure personalty, the declaration is also a disposition.

Grey v. Inland Revenue Commissioners (1960) H.L.

S transferred shares to trustees. A resulting trust thereby arose. S then orally directed the trustees to hold the shares on certain trusts; and some time later executed a deed of declaration of trust in the same terms and expressing that the shares had been held on those trusts since the date of the oral direction. It was held that the oral direction by S was a purported disposition of an equitable interest, and must therefore be in writing under section 53(1) (*c*) to be valid.

It will be recalled that a declaration of trust respecting an equitable interest in *land* must comply with section 53(1) (*b*). If it is also covered by the *Grey* v. *I.R.C.* interpretation of section 53(1) (*c*), the effect is to make that part of section 53(1) (*b*) redundant, since the requirement that the disposition declaration be in writing is much stiffer than that there be merely written evidence.

There is some confusion whether section 53(1) (*c*), following *Grey* v. *I.R.C.*, also applies where an equitable owner of pure personalty (and also land? subject again to the redundancy of section 53(1) (*b*)) declares himself a trustee thereof. If the sub-trust is passive, and the sub-trustee drops out, there is obviously a disposition, whatever the intention. The same equitable interest is shifted from one person to another, and as in *Grey* v. *I.R.C.* section 23(1) (*c*) must apply. However, if the sub-trust is active, there is merely the creation of a *new* equitable interest, the original interest remaining in the original equitable owner. Section 53(1) (*c*) does not apply. Some confusion may be caused by this distinction when an active sub-trust becomes a passive sub-trust. It is suggested that the applicability of section 53(1) (*c*) must be determined at the time of the declaration of trust. The fact that an active sub-trust might become a passive sub-trust must make no difference to the validity of the active sub-trust created without compliance with section 53(1) (*c*).

Section 53(2) Law of Property Act 1925 expressly provides that section 53 does not affect the creation or operation of resulting, implied or constructive trusts. The formalities dealt with are a prerequisite only in the valid creation of express trusts.

4. *Some further consideration of section 53(1) (c)*
Section 53(1) (*c*) requires that the disposition itself actually be in writing, not merely evidenced in writing. This implies that a failure to comply with section 53(1) (*c*) makes the purported disposition void.

It is not clear how far the phrase "disposition of an equitable interest or trust" extends. It clearly encompasses a direct assignment or transfer by a beneficiary of his

5. *The maxim: "Equity will not permit a statute to be used as an instrument of fraud"*

Courts exercising equitable jurisdiction, although bound by statute, will intervene in some cases to prevent fraud being done in reliance on a statute. The doctrine of part performance, discussed in land law textbooks, is an illustration.

In *Rochefoucauld* v. *Boustead* (1897) it was said to be "a fraud on the part of a person to whom land is conveyed as a trustee and who knows it was so conveyed, to deny the trust and claim the land himself." The setting up of a statute to achieve this end will not be permitted.

Hodgson v. Marks (1971) C.A.

P transferred a house to E, with an oral agreement that the house was to remain P's even though transferred to E. Ungoed-Thomas J. held that there could be no reliance by E or his successor in title, (even if a purchaser for value without notice?) on section 53(1) (*b*) Law of Property Act 1925 to defeat P's claim because this would be to permit a statute to be used as an instrument of fraud. The C.A. upheld a constructive trust, and applied section 53(2) to avoid formalities; but clearly also agreed with Ungoed-Thomas J.

The principle seems to have been replaced in practice in these cases by the automatic imposition of a constructive trust. See *Bannister* v. *Bannister* (1948); *Binions* v. *Evans* (1972); *Re Densham* (1975).

4 Express Trusts—
The Prerequisite of Complete Constitution; and Contracts to Create Trusts

For there to arise a "proper" and valid trust, there must be, apart from satisfaction of the prerequisites already discussed, *complete constitution*. Only then will there be, strictly speaking, a *cestui que trust* who can enforce the trust. Further, whether he is a volunteer or not will not matter (see below for discussion). He has his position of strength because of the trust.

The clearest expression of the relevant principles is in Turner L. J.'s judgment in *Milroy* v. *Lord* (1862). Complete constitution is defined as the rendering of a purely voluntary settlement valid and effectual, by the settlor's having "done everything which, according to the nature of the property comprised in the settlement, was necessary to be done in order to transfer the property and render the settlement binding upon him." As was seen in Chapter 3, there are two basic methods of declaring trusts.

1. *Declaration of self as trustee*
   In this case, whether the settlor has a legal (absolute) or equitable interest in property, an effective declaration is synonymous with complete constitution. There must be a clear irrevocable declaration, a question of certainty of intention. Note the discussion on formal requirements in Chapter 3.

Paul v. Constance (1977) C.A.

C separated from his wife D, and in 1967 started living with P as man and wife. C received a sum in damages in 1973. He and P decided to open a deposit account with the sum, which was in C's name alone. C constantly told P the money was hers as much as his. C died. It was held that in view of this relationship, the words of C could be construed as a declaration of trust by C of the sum for himself and P is equal shares.

Cf. Jones v. Lock (1865) Ch. Ct.

A father put a cheque into his baby son's hands and said: "I give this to baby; it is for himself, and I am going to put it away for him . . ." Lord Cranworth L.C. held, as a matter of fact, that this was a loose conversation whereby the father merely meant to say that he could now make a provision for the baby.

There can be an effective trust although the intended beneficiary knows nothing of it. See *Middleton* v. *Pollock* (1876).

2. *Declaration of trust by transfer to trustee*

Where the intending settlor is absolute owner of property (both at law and in equity) he must as a basic principle, vest the legal title in the intended trustee transferee. The requirements for the effective passing of the legal title vary with the property: *e.g.* land, freehold or leasehold, can only be transferred by deed; personal chattels can pass by delivery or deed of gift; registered shares only pass if the instrument of transfer is entered in the company's register (see *Milroy* v. *Lord*).

Where the intending settlor has only an equitable interest in property, a trust (*i.e.* sub-trust) of the equitable interest can be completely constituted by an *assignment* of the interest to intended trustees. Any such disposition must be in writing (s. 53(1) (*c*) L.P.A. 1925).

Kekewich v. Manning (1851) Ch. Ct.

Trustees held shares on trust for A for life, remainder to B absolutely. B executed a voluntary assignment of his equitable reversionary interest to C upon trust for D. A valid trust was thus created over the equitable interest; the legal title remained vested in the original trustees.

Note the way in which some declarations of trust over subsisting equitable interests may give rise to the *Grainge* v. *Wilberforce* dropping-out principle, already discussed under Chapter 3.

In *Milroy* v. *Lord*, it was also established that if an intending settlor evinces an intention to set up a trust by transferring the property to trustees, but fails to transfer effectively, the court will not read into the failed transfer an effective declaration of self as trustee. There will be no completion of the imperfect gift, or in this case, trust.

Richards v. Delbridge (1874) Ct. of Equity

J.D., a bone manure merchant, was assisted by his grandson E.R. J.D. endorsed and signed on the lease of his business premises a memorandum: "This deed and all thereto belonging I give to E.R. for this time forth, with all the stock-in-trade." J.D. delivered the lease to E.R.'s mother. On J.D.'s death, did the lease and business pass to E.R., or under J.D.'s will? It was held: (i) there was no effective conveyance to E.R.; (ii) the ineffective attempt to convey could not be read as a declaration of self as trustee by J.D. The property passed under J.D.'s will.

3. *The Re Rose gloss*

It is generally thought that *Re Rose* (1952) establishes that "although the legal title may remain vested in the settlor, an attempted transfer by him to a trustee may nevertheless be effective in equity and enable an enforceable trust to be established *where the settlor has done everything in his power* to divest himself of the property in favour of the trustee" (*per* P. H. Pettit, *Equity and the Law of Trusts*, 4th edit. 1979, p.67) (emphasis supplied).

Re Rose (1952) C.A.

On March 30, 1943, D executed, in respect of 10,000 shares, a transfer in proper form in favour of his wife and X as trustee. The share certificates were handed to the transferees. The legal title to the shares could only pass by an entry in the company's register, and the company's articles of association authorised the directors to refuse registration if they desired. In fact, the transfer was registered on June 30, 1943. D died on February 16, 1947; and whether or not estate duty was payable on the shares transferred on March 30, 1943 depended upon whether the transfer was effective before April 10, 1943. It was held that although the legal title did not pass until June 30, 1943, the transfer was effective on March 30, 1943, because D had "done all in his power to divest himself of and to transfer to the transferees the whole of his right, title and interest, legal and equitable, in the shares in question" (*per* Jenkins L. J.). Between March 30, 1943 and June 30, 1943, D was a trustee of the bare legal title for the transferees, and there was a sub-trust for the ultimate beneficiaries.

The doctrine is open to criticism. See (1976) 40 Conv. 139 (Lord McKay).

If D holds on a bare trust for the transferees, what would happen if the directors of the company refused to register any transfer to these transferees? The so-called trust would be unenforceable and worthless to both the transferees and the ultimate beneficiaries, at least without further radical interference from equity (*e.g.* the coerced registration of the transfer). It is simply unfortunate that a circumstance beyond D's control may thwart his detailed intentions. A trust should only arise when the transfer is properly registered, in accordance with the workable principles laid down in *Milroy* v. *Lord*. If *Re Rose* is not disregarded altogether, it should at the least be limited to the special case of share transfers.

The maxim: "Equity will not assist a volunteer"

The beneficiary under a *fully* constituted trust is, in equitable terms, not a volunteer, because he has available to him the full range of equitable remedies. There may, however, be situations in which there is *no* fully constituted trust, but where nevertheless the intended beneficiary has some remedy available to him. This is a very difficult area, and it is hoped that a somewhat lengthy treatment of it here will help settle the problems remaining in the reader's mind. Where the remedy sought is an equitable remedy—injunction or, more particularly, specific performance — the intended beneficiary must not be a volunteer in the eyes of equity. There may, alternatively, be available the common law remedy of damages even where the intended beneficiary is a volunteer in the eyes of equity. Whether or not an intended beneficiary is a volunteer is determined by the test of "consideration."

Does equity recognise the "consideration" he has offered? The following table may be of immediate use:

Equitable Remedy	Type of Consideration	Common Law Remedy
Specific performance/ Constructive trust	1. Marriage	None
Specific performance	2. Valuable (Contractual)	Damages
None	3. Deed/Seal	Damages

An understanding of valuable or contractual consideration, and of consideration by way of seal, should already have been achieved in a course on the law of contract. What is marriage consideration? This arises where a settlement or trust is agreed to be made *before* and in consideration of a marriage. Only certain persons can take advantage of this situation (are within the marriage consideration) — clearly, the husband, wife and actual issue of their marriage. Some

33

cases refer to other persons whose interests appear to be so entwined with the marriage that they are also regarded as within the class, there being no coherent way of separating them.

The situations to be discussed here are those where the declaration of a trust by an intended settlor takes the form of a valid contract to transfer property to trustees on trust. Any declaration of self as trustee would automatically give rise to a trust, except where the intended trust property is not in the ownership of the intending settlor. In such case, if a valid contract is made at the time of declaration, the same principles will apply. The contract can be between himself and the intended beneficiary of the trust; or between himself and the intended trustees of the trust; or between himself and a third party; or between himself and any mixture of these groupings. See, generally, (1979) Current Legal Problems 1 (C.E.F. Rickett).

1. *Contract between intending settlor and intended beneficiary*

If the contract to transfer on trust is a covenant under seal, the intended beneficiary may rely on his position as covenantee to obtain damages.

Cannon v. Hartley (1949) Ch. Div.

A daughter brought an action to obtain damages for an alleged breach of covenant by her father in refusing to settle, under the terms of that covenant, a reversionary interest in a residuary estate on trust for her. She succeeded. Romer J. stressed she could not obtain specific performance as she was a volunteer in the eyes of equity. It should be noted that the daughter's obtaining damages did not completely constitute the intended trust in her favour. She merely received in monetary damages the value of what she would have obtained had the contract been performed. Had she been able to obtain a decree of specific performance, this would have had the effect of being a coerced constitution of the intended trust.

Where the intended beneficiary has provided valuable consideration for the promise to transfer, he has in theory a remedy in damages or for specific performance. I have argued elsewhere at length (see (1979) C.L.P. 1, at pp. 2-3) that *Beswick* v. *Beswick* (1968) provides strong support for the argument that in cases of contracts to settle property on trust, specific performance will usually be granted because of the inadequacy of damages. This will effect a constitution of the intended trust.

2. *The doctrine of marriage consideration*

Through the doctrine of marriage consideration, equity attaches to *some* persons in the position of covenantee beneficiaries and, further, to others not actual parties to the covenant but nevertheless intended beneficiaries, the right to expect some form of *equitable* relief in their favour. These persons are those intended beneficiaries within the marriage consideration (see above). The equitable relief granted takes the form either of specific performance of the covenant to settle, or of declaration of a constructive trust over the property within the scope of the covenant once it falls into the hands of the convenantor, such trust being in the same terms as the intended express trust. The latter remedy, it is suggested, if always granted, seems to oust specific performance.

Pullan v. Koe (1913) Ch. Div.

A marriage settlement in 1859 contained a covenant by H and W with the trustees to settle W's after-acquired property worth £100 or more. In 1879 W received £285. She paid this into H's bank account. Part of the money was invested in bearer bonds. In 1909 H died, and the bonds were in his executors' possession. The trustees of the settlement brought an action against H's executors. Swinfen-Eady J. held that at the moment the wife received the money, which came within the covenant, it was bound under that covenant and was therefore subject in equity to a trust. The money could be traced into its product, the two bearer bonds, by the trustees.

What results does this doctrine have? First, in cases of covenants to settle in consideration of marriage, there is no need for a separate constitution where the beneficiaries include someone within the marriage consideation. The covenant is itself the constitution, because a trust will be imposed. Secondly, where the intended beneficiaries do not include someone within the marriage consideration, there is no-one in whose favour a constructive trust might be imposed. See *Re Plumptre's Marriage Settlement* (1910). This creates a confusing situation in cases where the court has not actually been asked to declare that a trust exists. If a trust would be deemed to exist the moment the property reached the hands of the convenantor-settlor, do next-of-kin volunteers obtain equitable interests at that moment? If so, they surely cannot be divested of their interests simply because the court has yet *to declare* that the trust has existed? The solution may be that the *Pullan* v. *Koe* constructive trust is rather more a remedy that a substantive institution. These divergent methods of dealing with constructive trusts will arise again in Chapter 7.

3. *The device of a trust of the promise*

This device supplies a method whereby an intended beneficiary has a reasonable expectation of some form of remedy *in his own right*, even though he is neither (a) a party to a covenant under seal to settle property on trust for himself; nor (b) a person who has provided valuable consideration for a promise to settle property on trust for himself; nor (c) a person who can rely on the doctrine of marriage consideration. The intending settlor has made a contract to create a trust, in favour of the intended beneficiary, with the intended trustee (or even with a third party). The latter intended trustee has a contractual right, a *chose in action*, against the intending settlor. The existence of a completely constituted trust of the promise means that the intended trustee's contractual right is held by him on trust for the intended beneficiary. The intended beneficiary of the intended trust of the property is in fact the constituted beneficiary of a completely constituted trust of the promise.

For a trust of the promise to arise there must be:

(a) a clearly manifested intention to set up such trust. See statements in *Re Schebsman* (1944), *Green* v. *Russell* (1959), *Vandepitte* v. *Preferred Accident Insurance Corp. of New York* (1933). *Cf. Fletcher* v. *Fletcher* (1844), using a more liberal 19th Century approach, which would probably be decided differently today.

(b) a promise capable of being the subject matter of a trust. See Buckley J. in *Re Cook's Settlement Trusts* (1965), who suggested that contractual promises to settle after-acquired property cannot be held on trust. This is a doubtful doctrine, and has been widely criticised by academic writers.

The nature of the contractual right being held on trust will vary with the type of contract. If there is merely a covenant, there will be only a right to damages. If there is a contract founded on valuable consideration, there is probably an action for specific performance.

The orthodox view on the effect of establishing a trust of the promise is summed up by Hanbury and Maudsley, *Modern Equity*, 10th edit., 1976, at p. 186: "Where a contractual right is held by A on trust for B, A may sue and obtain damages or a decree of specific performance on behalf of B (*Lloyd's* v. *Harper*, 1880); or B may obtain such relief on his own account if A refuses to act, joining A as co-defendant in the action (*Les Affreteurs Reunis Societe Anonyme* v. *Leopold Walford Ltd.*, 1919)." If the remedy granted is specific performance, the intended trust will in effect become completely constituted. If the remedy granted is damages, and these damages are paid to the intended trustee, they will be held on trust for the intended beneficiary. The intended trustee only gets substantial damages because he is suing on behalf of the intended beneficiary, or, alternatively, the constituted beneficiary of the trust of the promise.

I have not been able to agree with the orthodox view,

and have presented elsewhere an alternative view, based on constructive trusts. See (1979) C.L.P. 1.

4. *Where there is a contract between the intending settlor and the intended trustee, but where the intended beneficiary has no remedy in his own right under contract, marriage consideration or trust of the promise.*

Where there exists a trust of the promise, we have seen that the intended beneficiary of the intended trust of the property can *compel* the intended trustee to pursue his contractual remedies against the intending settlor, but on behalf of the intended beneficiary. A question now comes to mind: If there is no trust of the promise, may the intended trustee nevertheless pursue in his own right as a party to the contract to create a trust a contractual remedy which may have the effect of giving the intended beneficiary some remedy *in practice*? For instance, if the intended trustee were to obtain specific performance, the intended trust would be coercively constituted. If he were to obtain damages, those could be held on trust for the intended beneficiary in the same way as they are when there is a trust of the promise.

Three first instance decisions have provided some form of answer to this query. The cases are *Re Pryce* (1917), *Re Kay's Settlement* (1939) and *Re Cook's Settlement Trusts* (1965). It is suggested that they establish, when read together chronologically, a narrow equitable rule — an intended trustee *cannot* pursue any common law right to sue for damages for breach of a *covenant* to settle after-acquired property on trust for volunteers, including next-of-kin.

Re Pryce (1917) Ch. Div.

In a marriage settlement, the wife covenanted with the trustees to settle after-acquired property. Property brought into the settlement by the wife (including after-acquired property) was held on successive life interests to the wife and the husband, remainder to the children of the marriage (there were none), ultimate remainder to the wife's next-of-kin (volunteers). The husband was dead. The wife wished the covenant not to be enforced. The trustees of the settlement asked for directions, and Eve J. held they ought not to take any steps to compel the transfer to them of after-acquired property falling within the terms of the covenant. See criticism of *Pryce* in (1960) 76 L.Q.R. 100 (d. W. Elliott).

In *Re Kay* Simonds J., in following *Pryce*, went further than Eve J. and *directed* the trustees not to take any steps either to compel performance of the covenant or to recover damages through the covenantor's failure to perform the covenant.

Re Cook's Settlement Trusts (1965) Ch. Div.

Sir Francis Cook covenanted with the trustees of a re-settlement that if certain assets were sold, the proceeds of the sale would be paid to them on trust for his children (who were volunteers). Buckley J. cited *Pryce* and *Kay* in holding that the trustees ought not to seek a remedy against Sir Francis.

Students often find themselves in some confusion in this area because there has been a plethora of academic discussion and criticism of the three cases. The issue is essentially whether they are justified in principle. As the cases only deal with the situation where trustees apply to the court for directions, there is some hope that if they are not justified in principle, they will not be followed in the situation where the trustees choose to bring an action directly.

A common criticism is that in all three cases the court was wrong not to uphold a trust of the promise on behalf of the intended volunteer beneficiaries. Buckley J. in *Cook* answered this by asserting that a promise to settle after-acquired property *cannot* be the subject matter of a trust. This holding has itself been widely criticised. The real answer to the criticism is that in none of the cases was there ever an unambiguous intention to establish a trust of the promise. A further argument is that wherever next-of-kin are the beneficiaries involved, there should be *automatically*, regardless of any test of intention, a trust of the promise. This comes too close to an unwarranted extension of marriage consideration.

What *positive* reasons are offered for the equitable rule?

1. Equity will not assist a volunteer directly, so that it will not assist him indirectly either, by allowing his trustee to sue (in effect on the beneficiary's behalf).

2. Equity will do nothing in vain. Where an intended trustee sues under a trust of the promise he can obtain substantive damages, which will then be held on trust for the intended beneficiary — here equity is not acting in vain. Where, however, an intended trustee sues on his own behalf, he has suffered no real loss and can obtain only nominal damages — to allow him to sue would be acting in vain.

3. Equity will do nothing in vain. Even if a non trust of the promise intended trustee is awarded substantial damages, there is nothing to link him with the non trust of the promise intended beneficiary, because there is no trust of the promise. Clearly, the trustee cannot have the damages for himself. He must hold them on resulting trust for the settlor, the very person from whom he recovered them. There is thus no point in letting him sue.

These orthodox defences of principle have each found their champions. I am not among them, and have argued another, more embracing rationale for the rule. See (1979) C.L.P. 1, at pp. 10-13.

4. Equity turns its face against corruption. "Where there is no trust of the promise, the beneficial interest in the liberty to sue vests in (the intended trustee). (The intended beneficiary) has no rights in relation to (the intended trustees') pursuing an action on the contract. (The intended trustee) is not compellable. He is free to do as he wishes. In effect, he is free to constitute the

intended trust if he can obtain specific performance; or he is free to claim substantial damages upon which a trust for (the intended beneficiary) will immediately be imposed. It is this position of power which lies at the root of equity's refusal to allow a legally non-compellable intended trustee to pursue his contractual remedies. It gives rise to a very real possibility of corruption, in the form of inducements from various quarters to sue or not to sue" (*op. cit.* at pp. 12-13).

It must be noticed that proposition 4 provides support for an equitable rule which is much wider than that actually established in *Pryce*, *Kay* and *Cook*. "Where (the intended trustee) does not hold his contractual rights (whether by virtue of covenant or contract for value) on trust for (the intended beneficiary), he (the intended trustee) will not be allowed to pursue a common law claim in damages, or possibly even a claim for specific performance" (*op. cit.* at p. 10).

5. *Where there is a contract to create a trust between the intending settlor and a third party*

Can a contracting third party, who is not the intended trustee, rely on his contract to obtain either specific performance or damages (which presumably will be held by the third party on trust for the intended beneficiary)? There is no clear authority. It is suggested that, in view of the wide-ranging nature of proposition 4 above, he could not. His position is, like that of a non trust of the promise trustee, one of considerable strength which again gives rise to possibilities of corruption, etc. (*Op. cit.* at pp. 13-14).

6. *Complete constitution of trusts based upon unenforceable contracts*

If a settlor has in fact transferred property to trustees in performance of an unenforceable contract (on the above analysis) to settle the property in favour of volunteers, the trust is completely constituted. The trustees hold the property on the declared trusts. The volunteer beneficiaries

41

have constituted equitable interests. The settlor has no claim for the return of the property.

Paul v. Paul (1882) C.A.

Under a marriage settlement, W's property was settled on H and W for life, remainder to the children (there were none); in default of children, if W survived for her absolutely; if H survived, as W should by will appoint; in default of appointment for the next-of-kin excluding H. H and W separated. W tried to recover from the trustees the remaining capital in the settlement. She failed, because the trust had been constituted. The next-of-kin were volunteers, but they also had interests as *cestuis que trust*. See also *Re Bowden* (1936).

Re Ralli's Will Trusts (1964) Ch. Div.

This difficult case repays some close analysis. A testator, who died in 1899, left his residue on trust for his wife for life, and then to his daughters H and I absolutely. In 1924 H in her marriage settlement covenanted to settle all her existing and after-acquired property on trusts which failed and ultimately on trust for I's children (volunteers). The settlement declared that "all the property comprised within the terms of such (covenant) shall become subject in equity to the settlement hereby covenanted to be made thereof." P, I's husband, was one of the settlement trustees. In 1946 P was appointed a trustee of the original testator's will. In 1956 H died. In 1961 the testator's widow died. P was the sole surviving trustee of both the will and the settlement. The question was: did P hold H's share of the testator's residue on trust for H's estate under the trusts of the will, or on the trusts of H's marriage settlement? Buckley J. made two findings. (1) The declaration in the settlement showed that H intended herself to become a trustee of any property she received which was within the terms of the covenant to settle, but which had not yet been transferred to the trustees. There was thus a completely constituted trust of the property, in the terms of the marriage settlement. The rule that equity will not assist a volunteer to enforce an executory contract to make a settlement had no application in the case. (2) The property had in any case become subject to trusts of the settlement, because the trustee of that settlement P now had an effective legal title to the property, although his title had reached him (fortuitously) because he was also trustee of the testator's will. No party had an equity against P disentitling him to stand upon his legal right. H could not have done so, because she was bound by the solemn covenant. Her successors in title were also bound. To make good a claim to the property H's successors in title (the defendants) "must show that the plaintiff cannot conscientiously withold it from them. When they seek to do this, he can point to the covenant which . . . relieves him from any fiduciary obligation he would otherwise owe to the defendants as H's representatives. In so doing the plaintiff is not seeking to enforce an equitable remedy against the defendants on behalf of persons who could not enforce such a remedy themselves: he is relying upon the combined effect of his legal ownership of the fund and his right under the covenant." Therefore the property was held subject to the settlement, and the volunteer children of I had a good equity against P. The fortuitous vesting of the property in the trustee, coupled with a careful balancing of the merits of each interested party's claim, had in effect constituted the trusts of the settlement.

Recognised exceptions to the maxim: "Equity will not assist a volunteer"

1. *The rule in Strong v. Bird (1874)*

2. *Donatio mortis causa*

3. *Statutory exceptions*

4. *Proprietary estoppel*

5 Secret Trusts

The paradigm case of a *fully secret trust* occurs where a
testator has left his property *by his will* to A absolutely,
apparently for A's own benefit; but where during his
lifetime the testator has informed A that he was not to take
the property beneficially, but was to hold it on certain
trusts, and A had agreed to this. The paradigm case of a
half secret trust occurs where the will declares on its face
that A is to hold the property on trust, but does not express
the terms of the trust.

A fully secret trust may also arise where a person dies
intestate, but had received an undertaking from that person
entitled to his property in the event of his death intestate
that he would hold the property on trust.

Secret trusts offer particular advantages of, as their name
implies, secrecy. Wills are public documents open to
inspection. By setting up a secret trust, therefore, a
testator is able to keep out of the public eye the objects of
his bounty.

1. *The justifications for the enforcement of secret trusts*
Section 9 of the Wills Act 1837 states:

> "No will shall be valid unless it shall be in writing
> and . . . signed at the foot or end thereof by the
> testator, or by some other person in his presence and
> by his direction; and such signature shall be made or
> acknowledged by the testator in the presence of two
> or more witnesses present at the same time, and such
> witnesses shall attest and shall subscribe the will in the
> presence of the testator, but no form of attestation
> shall be necessary."

The purpose of the section is obvious — "to ensure that false claims cannot be generated after the death of a testator when he is in no position to refute them." (*per* A. J. Oakley, *Constructive Trusts*, 1978, at p. 86). The issue of justification is centred on this provision: *why* do the courts enforce dispositions of property which do not comply with the statutory requirements for such dispositions? Why do the courts allow an alternative method of disposition? This is the question of the motives of the court. The issue of justification has a second strand, which is too often confused with the first: *how* do the courts enforce such dispositions without flying in the face of the statute? How do the courts fit in an alternative method of disposition in a situation where the statute has a *prima facie* monopoly? This is the question of mechanical operation of the trust.

The motives of the court

This matter must be looked at chronologically. To begin with fully secret trusts were the only type to be asserted, probably because there was available a strong argument which appealed to the courts. If the court relied too much on the letter of the Wills Act, so as to prevent the introduction of evidence which might establish the testator's true intentions for his property, and the agreement of the *prima facie* absolute beneficiary to these proposals, this would be allowing the Wills Act to be used as an instrument of fraud. The beneficiary under the will would be able to disregard his undertaking to the testator and take the property for himself. See Chapter 2 for further discussion of the maxim: "Equity will not allow a statute to be used as an instrument of fraud."

McCormick v. Grogan (1869) H.L.

A testator made a will leaving all his property to Grogan. When about to die, he summoned Grogan, and told him a letter would be found with the will. He obtained no undertaking from Grogan. The letter named several persons

45

to whom he wished Grogan to give money, but he left
Grogan a complete discretion in the matter. Lord Hatherley
L.C. said the doctrine of secret trusts had only been applied
in "cases in which the Court has been persuaded that there
has been a fraudulent inducement held out on the part of
the apparent beneficiary in order to lead the testator to
confide to him the duty which he so undertook to
perform." This basis required, before a trust could be
established, that Grogan "knew that the testator or the
intestate was beguiled and deceived by his conduct." There
had been no fraud on Grogan's part, and thus there was no
legally binding obligation upon Grogan.

There is still some hangover from the prevention of
fraud motive in relation to the standard of proof required
to set up a trust. In *McCormick* v. *Grogan* it was said to
need the clearest and most indisputable evidence. However,
in *Ottaway* v. *Norman* (1972) Brightman J. said only "clear
evidence" was necessary; while in *Re Snowden* (1979)
Megarry V.C. has introduced a distinction between cases
based on fraud — which require a high standard of proof
because of the gross moral nature of fraud — and cases not
based on fraud — which require an ordinary civil standard
of proof.

The discussion thus far reveals an important factor
which needs to be grasped. The actual detailed rules of
secret trusts (to be discussed herein) reflect the arguments
the courts have used to justify their enforcement, and it is
this factor which explains the contradictory nature of
many rules relating to fully secret trusts on the one hand,
and to half secret trusts on the other.

An issue was bound to arise: with enforcement of
fully secret trusts, why not also half secret trusts? However,
in a half secret trust there was no possible fraud on the part
of the named legatee. He could not take beneficially since
he was named as a trustee — he would hold the property on
a resulting trust for the testator's estate in the event of a
failure of the expressed trust.

Blackwell v. Blackwell (1929) H.L.

A testator gave £12,000 to five named persons, the income to be applied "for the purposes indicated by me to them," with power to apply £8,000 of the capital "to such person or persons indicated by me to them" as they saw fit. The objects of the trust were communicated orally to the trustees, and accepted by them before the will was executed. The half secret trust was upheld, the Law Lords holding that the general doctrine concerning the enforcement of fully secret trusts extended to the case of a trust on the face of the will where the trustee-legatee was acting with perfect honesty, and only desired to do "what in other circumstances the Court would have fastened it on their conscience to perform."

The enforcement of half secret trusts indicates a shift in the motives of the court, from the negative one of preventing fraud by imposing a secret trust, to the positive one of encouraging the performance of the testator's true revealed intention if at all possible. It was seen that the Wills Act aims to prevent disputes which a testator cannot deal with himself. He can make his intentions clear in a secure form. Likewise secret trusts are enforced because the court wishes to see the testator's revealed intentions carried out.

The mechanical operation of the trust

While fully secret trusts were based on the prevention of fraud, the courts needed to give no explanation of how they manoeuvred past the Wills Act. They simply disregarded it in applying a standard general equitable maxim. However, in *Blackwell* v. *Blackwell* the Wills Act cropped up. Viscount Sumner laid the foundation of the principle that secret trusts do not conflict with the Wills Act because they operate outside it. "It is communication of the purpose to the legatee, coupled with acquiescence or promise on his part, that removes the matter from the provision of the Wills Act and brings it within the law of trusts, as applied in this instance to trustees, who happen

also to be legatees." Secret trusts operate wholly outside
the will in question and so are governed not by the rules
of probate but by the rules of the law of trusts. Oral
evidence to establish a trust is thus permitted.

The will does, however, have a role to play. It is the
instrument through which the trust is completely
constituted and thus becomes valid. The rules of probate
will govern the vesting of the property in the secret trustee/
legatee; while the law of trusts governs any issue concerning
the operation of the secret trust. Some cases indicate that
this general distinction is valid.

Re Young (1951) Ch. Div.

One of the beneficiaries under a half secret trust
attested the will. Section 15 Wills Act 1837 provides that a
legacy to an attesting witness is invalid. The law of trusts
does not prohibit the signing of the trust deed by the
trustees or the beneficiaries. The court held that the trust
arose outside the will, and section 15 was irrelevant. The
beneficiary could take.

Cf., however, if a fully secret trustee attested the will,
the legacy to him must be ineffective, and the trust would
fail. If a half secret trustee attested the will, the legacy to
him would still be effective, and the trust would come into
existence.

Re Maddock (1902) C.A.

A dictum was to the effect that if a fully secret trustee
predeceased the testator the legacy will lapse *because of* his
decease prior to the testator (see *Re Smirthwaite's Trusts*,
1871).

Re Gardner (No. 2) (1923) Ch. Div.

Romer J. held that a beneficiary under a secret trust
acquired an interest as soon as the trust was communicated
to and accepted by the secret trustee. His death prior to
that of the testator meant that his beneficial interest passed
to his personal representatives. The decision is wrong. A

beneficiary under a trust has no interest until the trust is completely constituted, which, in the case of a secret trust, means the vesting of the property in the secret trustee at the death of the testator.

What happens if a secret trustee disclaims his legacy? The court has a statutory, and inherent, power to appoint a trustee to act in the place of a trustee who declines to act. Thus, if a half secret trustee disclaims the legacy, the court will probably appoint another person to act in his stead. If, on the other hand, a fully secret trustee disclaims his legacy, the legacy must fail altogether because he is beneficially entitled under the will. There is a conflict of views on this point (*Blackwell* v. *Blackwell*, 1929).

It would appear that all secret trusts *operate* outside the will in question, although the constitution of the trust property depends upon the operation of the will. Coupled with the positive motive the court has in enforcing secret trusts, it is suggested that in principle all secret trusts are express trusts.

2. *Secret trusts: express trusts or not?*

A question is perpetually posed. Are secret trusts express or constructive? It will be remembered that section 53(1) Law of Property Act 1925 requires certain formalities for the creation of express trusts, but such formalities are not required for constructive trusts, section 53(2). Some cases provide clues, but are essentially indecisive.

Re Baillie (1886) Ch. Ct.

A half secret trust of land was not effective because the necessary writing was absent. Half secret trusts are express?

Ottaway v. Norman (1972) Ch. Div.

A fully secret trust relating to land was upheld, even though there was no writing. There was no argument about formalities, and the decision suggests that fully secret trusts are thus constructive.

On arguments of principle it was suggested above that *all* secret trusts are express trusts, and must thus comply with section 53(1) L.P.A. 1925. If, however, the prevention of fraud motive is foremost in the enforcement of *fully* secret trusts, there is no reason why they ought not to be classified as constructive trusts.

Some might claim that if fully secret trusts are express, a secret trustee might therefore be able to profit by arguing that the absence of writing invalidates any secret trust and he must take beneficially. This is not so. A constructive trust will then be imposed based on the general maxim: "Equity will not permit a statute to be used as an instrument of fraud." See *Bannister* v. *Bannister* (1948). The constructive trust that is imposed is not, however, the express secret trust (which has failed), even though both trusts have the same terms.

In *Nichols* v. *I.R.C.* (1973) there was a suggestion that the doctrine of secret trusts applied to both testamentary and *inter vivos* gifts. *Bannister* v. *Bannister* is sometimes cited as an *inter vivos* express trust. However, the view of Pennycuick J. in *Re Tyler's Fund Trusts* (1967) is preferred: "It is probably true to say that the particular principles of law applicable to secret trusts are really concerned only with trusts created by will." This view reflects the positive reasons the courts have for enforcing expressed secret trusts.

3. *The requirements of fully secret trusts*
   (a) The legatee must take the property as beneficial owner on the face of the will. Phrases which establish no legal obligation on him, but a mere moral obligation, do not matter.
   (b) It must be proved that the testator did actually communicate the trust during his lifetime to the legatee/devisee; and that the latter expressly or impliedly accepted it. Silence is assent.
   (*Wallgrave* v. *Tebbs*, 1855)
   The trust may be communicated and accepted either before or after the date of the will, but it

must be before the death of the testator.
(*Moss* v. *Cooper*, 1861)

The communication and acceptance may be made
constructively, *e.g.* by a sealed envelope. (*Re Boyes*,
1884; *cf. Re Keen*, 1937; *Re Bateman's Will
Trusts*, 1970)

(c) If a legatee accepts a fully secret trust during the
testator's lifetime, but there is no express or
constructive communication of the terms of the
trust during his lifetime, the trust will not take
effect. Instead, the trustee will hold the property
for the residuary legatee/devisee, or, with no gift
of residue, in favour of these entitled on intestacy
(*Re Boyes*). Alternatively, if the legatee does not
hear of the existence of the secret trust until after
the testator's death, he will take the property
beneficially, regardless of proof of a contrary
intention (*Wallgrave* v. *Tebbs*).

(d) There seems no reason why a fully secret trustee
cannot also be a beneficiary under the trust.

(e) Re Stead (1900) Ch. Div.

This case lays down the rules applying where a
testator leaves a legacy to two or more persons
jointly, but fails to communicate the trust to them
all. If the property is left to the legatees as *tenants
in common,*only those legatees to whom the trust
has been communicated are bound by it — the
others take their shares beneficially. If the
property is left to the legatees as *joint tenants*,
then if the testator has communicated with any of
the legatees prior to the execution of the will, all
the legatees are bound by the trust; on the other
other hand, if the testator does not communicate
with any of the legatees until after the execution
of the will, only those with whom he does
communicate are bound — the others take their
shares beneficially. See (1972) 85 L.Q.R. 225
(B. Perrins) for a detailed analysis of this case;

also a suggestion that the only question is whether the gift to *all* the legatees was induced by the agreement to act of any of them; if it was, *all* are bound; but if not then only those who have agreed are bound, and the others take beneficially.

4. *The requirements of half secret trusts*

Cf. cases where the probate doctrine of incorporation by reference arises — where property is left to a legatee for the purposes contained in a named existing and identifiable document, which then becomes part of the will. Where there is no document, or one which is not identifiable, there may be a half secret trust.

(a) The legatee must take the property as a trustee on the face of the will.

(b) Only such communications as are permitted by the terms of the trust. See dicta in *Blackwell* v. establish the terms of the trust. If the will refers to prior communications, then communications after the will's execution are not admissible (see *Re Keen*, 1937), but *cf.* point (d) below. Also *Re Spence* (1949).

(c) Where the trust is communicated before or at the same time as the execution of the will, evidence is admissible to show the terms of the trust, and the trustee is bound by the trust (see *Blackwell* v. *Blackwell*).

(d) It is apparently the case that any communications made after the execution of the will but before the testator's death are not admissible to show the terms of the trust. See *dicta* in *Blackwell* v. *Blackwell*; Lord Wright M.R. in *Re Keen* (although the case may properly have been decided under point (b) above); *Re Bateman's Will Trusts* (1970); *Johnson* v. *Ball* (1851). This rule has been widely criticised, and it has been suggested that future communications ought, in line with fully secret trusts, to be admissible.

(e) The legatee must accept the trust either before or contemporaneously with the execution of the will. Silence is acceptance. Acceptance may be express or constructive (see *Re Keen; Re Bateman's Will Trusts*).

(f) What happens when a testator leaves a legacy to two or more persons jointly as trustees, but fails to communicate with all of them? It is probable that the principles of *Re Stead* govern this situation as well, and determine which trustees hold on a half secret trust and which on trust for the residuary legatee or intestate successor.

(g) If the secret trust fails, the legatee will hold not beneficially but either for the residuary legatee or the intestate successor. (*Re Pugh's Will Trusts*, 1967). There seems no reason why, in this situation, he should not take beneficially as residuary legatee or intestate successor.

(h) A half secret trustee cannot be one of the secret beneficiaries, because, it is argued, the express provision of the will is that he take only as trustee. This is not convincing if the trust operates outside the will. (*Re Rees' Will Trusts*, 1950; *cf. Re Tyler's Fund Trusts*, 1967).

(i) If the testator asks the legatee to hold a particular sum on trust, but leaves a larger sum, only the original sum will be subject to the express trust, and the remainder will be held on trust for the residuary legatee or intestate successor. (*Re Colin Cooper*, 1939).

6 Implied and Resulting Trusts

The previous five chapters have been concerned with express trusts — where the settlor has expressed his intention to set up a trust. Some express trusts can be described as implied, *e.g.* where a settlor's intention is not clear and has to be gleaned from his conduct and general words. These are not covered in this chapter. Neither are mutual wills.

Many commentators view implied trusts as being synonymous with resulting trusts, since the implied intention of the settlor seems to play an important justificatory role in the doctrine of resulting trusts. There are essentially three cases:

(i) Where a man purchases property and has it conveyed or transferred into the name of another or the joint names of himself and another, when the beneficial interest will usually *result* to the man who put up the purchase money — PURCHASE IN THE NAME OF ANOTHER.

(ii) Where there is a voluntary conveyance or transfer into the name of another or into the joint names of the grantor and another, where the beneficial interest will usually *result* to the grantor — VOLUNTARY CONVEYANCE.

(iii) Where there is a transfer of property to another on trusts which leave some or all of the equitable interest undisposed of — FAILURE TO EXHAUST THE BENEFICIAL INTEREST.

It is said that in each of these cases the implied intention of the settlor/grantor must be that the property reverts back to himself. However, Underhill (*Law of Trusts and Trustees*, 12th edit., p. 11) classifies resulting trusts in two ways:

    (i) Where the resulting trust depends upon the presumed or implied intention of the grantor (essentially express trusts) — covers cases (a) and (b) above, and also (c) only where a trust has been established but there has been no attempt to dispose of the beneficial interest at all.

    (ii) Where a resulting trust comes into being without any question of intention, *e.g.* where a trust fails for uncertainty or because of illegality (essentially constructive trusts).

There has been some helpful judicial discussion on the issue of classification. In *Re Vandervell's Trusts (No. 2)* (1974) Megarry J. saw cases (a) and (b) above as *"presumed resulting trusts"*, resting on the intention of the grantor. However, he classified cases under (c) as *"automatic resulting trusts"*, because there is no issue of intention — it is merely the automatic outcome of the transferor's failure to dispose of what is vested in him. Megarry J. did not discuss express versus constructive, and appears to have viewed resulting trusts as an independent species. This is important because it alleviates cases (a), (b) and (c) from having to satisfy the formalities requirements of section 53(1) (*c*) Law of Property Act 1925 (see s. 53(2)). *Cf.* the results of Underhill's classification.

1. *Resulting Trusts — Purchase in the name of another*
    Wherever a person buys real or personal property and orders it conveyed, registered or otherwise transferred into the name of another, or of himself and another jointly, the court *presumes* that the other holds the property on trust for the person who has paid the purchase money. See Eyre C.B. in *Dyer* v. *Dyer* (1788), cited in *Pettitt* v. *Pettitt* (1969) *per* Lord Upjohn.

Bull v. Bull (1955) C.A.

A mother and son provided money in unequal shares for the purchase of a house, which was put in the son's name. The son claimed to be entitled solely, but the court decided he held as a trustee in favour of the mother and himself, taking as tenants in common in shares proportionate to their contributions. (*Cf.* where they contribute equally, they probably take as joint tenants in equity).

The presumption of a resulting trust applies equally to cases of husband and wife, especially cases concerning the ownership of the matrimonial home. (*Cf.* wide descretions given to courts to determine the division of matrimonial property in the event of the breakdown of the marriage, Matrimonial Causes Act 1973). The presumption of resulting trust can itself be rebutted by appropriate evidence to the contrary, indicating that a gift was clearly intended (see below); or the presumption of advancement might rebut the presumption of resulting trust (see below).

2. *Resulting Trusts — Voluntary conveyances*

A distinction is drawn between conveyances of land, and transfers of pure personalty.

(a) Land

The Law of Property Act 1925, section 60(3) provides:

> "In a voluntary conveyance a resulting trust for the grantor shall not be implied merely by reason that the property is not expressed to be conveyed for the use or benefit of the grantee".

Section 205(1) (xx) defines "property" as including any interest in real or personal property, unless the context requires otherwise. The use of the word "conveyance" in section 60(3) suggests that that section operates only in cases of interests in land.

Although there is some ambiguity in the matter, it is generally thought that, since 1925, in the absence of evidence to the contrary, there will be no resulting trust on a voluntary conveyance of land to another. However, where a conveyance is into the joint names of the grantor and another, there may be a strong case for a resulting trust to arise (*cf. Re Vinogradoff*, below).

(b) Pure personalty

There is authority for the proposition that if A transfers pure personalty into the names of A and B, there is a resulting trust for A.

Re Vinogradoff (1935) Ch. Div.

A testatrix, during her lifetime, transferred £800 War Loan into the joint names of herself and her infant grand-daughter aged four years. It was held that the grand-daughter held the War Loan on a resulting trust for the testatrix's estate.

The position is less clear if A voluntarily transfers pure personalty to B alone. In *George v. Howard* (1819) Richards C.B. thought there would not be a resulting trust; but in *Fowkes v. Pascoe* (1875) the C.A. in Chancery thought there would be. The latter, in view of *Re Vinogradoff*, seems the more sensible view.

Vandervell v. I.R.C. (1967) H.L.

V wished to found a Chair at the Royal College of Surgeons. Shares in V. Ltd. were transferred to the R.C.S., with an option to purchase the shares vested in T. Co., a trustee company. Dividends were declared in favour of R.C.S., and then T. Co. exercised the option with money belonging to the children of V. It was held that while the R.C.S. had been the legal owners of the shares, the beneficial ownership had remained in V by a resulting trust, because of the existence of the option to purchase. He was therefore liable to surtax on the dividends. Very little weight was actually attached to a *presumption* of a resulting trust. Lord Upjohn said he would have come to the same decision by simply looking at the facts, and referred to the presumption as "no more than a long-stop."

The presumption of a resulting trust in this case can be rebutted by clear evidence of a contrary intention, or by operation of the presumption of advancement.

3. Resulting Trusts — Rebutting the presumption in cases 1 and 2

The presumption of resulting trust only applies in the absence of sufficient evidence to the contrary. A presumed intention must give way to a true intention established by evidence. The intention to be established must be that at the date of the purchase or of the voluntary conveyance — and once a gift has been made, it cannot later be denied.

In *Cowcher* v. *Cowcher* (1972) Bagnell J. recognised two clear cases:

(a) Where land is conveyed to A, and the purchase money is given as to two-thirds by A and one-third by B, there is a resulting trust for B as to one-third unless there is a contrary intention, that is of B to *give* to A.

(b) Alternatively, in case (a) the established intention may be to create a trust in equal shares. Although there is a trust, it is express and not resulting, because of proposed beneficial shares different from the shares of the purchase price. Such trust must thus comply with section 53(1) (*b*) Law of Property Act 1925.

Fowkes v. Pascoe (1875) C.A. in Ch.

Mrs Baker purchased stock in her own name and in the name of her daughter-in-law's son (*not* Mrs Baker's grandson — hence no question of advancement). The court held that the intention was that Mrs Baker should receive the income during her life (*i.e.* that there was only in this respect a resulting trust), but that the property should belong to the step-grandson after her death (*i.e.* as to the remainder the resulting trust had been rebutted).

See also cases of money paid into a bank account in joint names — *Young* v. *Sealey* (1949); *Re Figgis* (1968).

Smith v. Cooke (1891) H.L.

Partners in a business assigned their assets to trustees to divide among their creditors. There was no provision about a surplus. There was a surplus. Was there a resulting trust for the partners? It was held there was no resulting trust since the trust deed had effectively disposed of all interest in the property. It was to be divided among the creditors, rather than to pay them.

Re Foord (1922) Ch. Div.

A bequest read: "I leave all my property to my sister absolutely in trust to pay my wife £300 per annum." Who was entitled to the surplus — the sister or the next-of-kin as resulting beneficiaries? Sargent J. held the sister to be entitled, for three reasons. The gift was to the sister "absolutely;" the gift was to her *qua* sister, not trustee; some of the property given was not income-producing at all.

4. *Resulting Trusts — Presumption of advancement in cases 1 and 2*

The presumption of advancement arises where property is put into the name of, or given to, or purchased for another, and where equity considers that there is an obligation imposed on the donor *to support* the donee. This presumption displaces the presumption of resulting trust. The presumption of advancement can itself be rebutted in whole or in part by sufficient contrary evidence, and the presumption of resulting trust reinstated.

Advancement occurs in cases of husband and wife, and parent and child.

(a) Husband and wife

When H puts property into W's name, it becomes hers. The presumption is that W is incapable of looking after herself, and therefore there is an obligation for H to do so.

Complex questions concerning the matrimonial home now tend to prevail.

Property rights are determined at the time of purchase or transfer, and these can only subsequently be altered if there is an agreement between the parties. Lord Upjohn in *Pettitt* v. *Pettitt* (1969) stated: "In the first place, the beneficial ownership of the property in question must depend on the agreement of the parties determined at the time of its acquisition. If the property in question is land there must be some lease or conveyance which shows how it was acquired. If that document declares not merely in whom the legal title is to vest but in whom the beneficial title is to vest that necessarily concludes the question of title as between the spouses for all time [unless varied by a subsequent agreement?], and in the absence of fraud or mistake at the time of the transaction the parties cannot go behind it at any time thereafter even on death or the breakup of the marriage . . . . But the document may be silent as to the beneficial title . . . . If there is no . . . available evidence then what are called the presumptions come into play."

The strength of the presumption of advancement has been considerably diminished as a result of statements from several Law Lords in *Pettit* v. *Pettit* and *Gissing* v. *Gissing* (1970). Lords Upjohn and Diplock, in particular, have stressed the changing conditions of society which make a 19th century presumption, itself based on the facts that husbands commonly made gifts to their wives, and that wives were economically dependent on their husbands, essentially obsolete. However, *Gissing* v. *Gissing* did establish that the presumption may still be of use in cases where there is no evidence at all of an agreement between the parties, because the courts will not invent an agreement where the parties did not make one, or where one cannot be inferred from their words and conduct.

  (i) *Purchase or transfer by H into the name of W, or into
      the joint names of H and W*
      It has always been possible to rebut the

presumption of advancement by evidence that no gift was intended (*e.g. Re Salisbury-Jones*, 1938); and, after *Pettit* and *Gissing* the presumption has little role to play.

Cf. Tinker v. Tinker (1970) C.A.

H, on purchasing the matrimonial home, had it conveyed into W's name, to avoid its being taken if his business failed. He acted honestly. The evidence of his intention was held to support a presumption of advancement. H thus could not claim the house on the break-up of the marriage, even though W had contributed nothing to its purchase.

(ii) *Purchase or transfer by W into the name of H, or into the joint names of W and H.*
There is no presumption of advancement, and H holds on resulting trust for W. See *Heseltine* v. *Heseltine* (1971)

(iii) *Contributions by both H and W to the purchase price of the property.*
Where there has been a divorce or break-up, it is seldom necessary to decide the exact property rights of H and W. Normally the matter can and should be dealt with under the Matrimonial Causes Act 1973, which enables the court to do what is just having ragard to all the circumstances. Even where the Act does not apply, it is likely that the courts will approach the determination of property rights in a discretionary manner. It is unlikely that Bagnall J.'s judgment in *Cowcher* v. *Cowcher* (1972),which was based on correct principles of trust and property law, will have much effect.

(b) **Parent and Child**
A gift from a father to his legitimate child raises the presumption of advancement (*Re Roberts*, 1946). As

regards mother to legitimate child, there is some confusion. *Bennet* v. *Bennet* (1879) gives a wavering interpretation, but suggests that in some situations, a presumption may arise based on a moral obligation owed by the mother to the child. In view of the social conditions of today, it is suggested that a presumption of advancement should arise as a matter of course. The presumption clearly arises in situations where a person has assumed a responsibility for another in a familial way, *i.e.* in *loco parentis* (see *Re Paradise Motor Co.*, 1968).

The presumption may be rebutted, and indeed the weaker the relationship, probably the weaker the presumption.

Warren v. Gurney (1944) C.A.

A father retained the title deeds of property he had given to his daughter. This was treated as conclusive in rebutting the presumption.

(c) Shepherd v. Cartwright (1955) H.L.

This case deals with the admissibility of evidence to rebut the presumption. First, the acts and declarations of the parties before or at the time of the transaction are available as evidence in all circumstances. This includes acts after but so immediately close to the transaction as to be in reality a part of the transaction. Secondly, subsequent acts and declarations are only available as evidence against their maker.

5. *Resulting Trust — Failure to exhaust the beneficial interest*

"Where a settlor transfers or conveys property to trustees, but fails to declare the trusts upon which it is to be held; or where the expressed trusts fail altogether on the ground, for instance, of uncertainty; or where they fail partially on similar grounds, or because the trusts expressed only dispose of a part of the equitable interest; in any such case the entire equitable interest, or such part thereof as has not been effectively disposed of, remains vested in the settlor or, in technical language, is said to result to him, and the property is accordingly said to be held by the trustees upon a resulting trust for him," or for his estate. (*per* P. H. Pettit, *Equity and the Law of Trusts*, 4th edit., p. 123). These trusts are referred to by Megarry J. in *Re Vandervell's Trusts (No. 2)* as "automatic resulting trusts." A resulting trust also arises where in a devise or bequest by a testator to trustees upon trusts, the latter fail altogether or in part. The resulting trust will be for those entitled to the residue; or, if it is a gift of the residue which fails, or there is no gift of residue, it will be for those persons entitled on intestacy.

There may be a complete failure of the alleged trust.

Essery v. Cowlard (1884) Ch. Div.

E, wishing to marry T, made an ante-nuptial settlement by which he gave property to trustees limited to the issue of the marriage. The marriage never took place, but there were children of the union. Pearson J. held that the marriage could not now take place, and even if it did take place the intention in the settlement would be frustrated (before 1926 there was no legitimation by subsequent marriage, and the issue of the union could not take as issue of the marriage).

There may be trusts, which are nevertheless improperly expressed.

Re Pugh's Will Trusts (1967) Ch. Div.

A testator left his residuary estate on trust, but did not define the objects of the trust. The property therefore passed to those entitled on the testator's intestacy.

There may be trusts, but which ultimately fail leaving a surplus.

Re the Trusts of the Abbott Fund (1900) Ch. Div.

A fund was raised by subscription to maintain and

support two distressed ladies. After the death of the survivor, there was a surplus. It was held that the surplus was held on resulting trust for the subscribers. See also *Re Gillingham Bus Disaster Fund* (1958).

Re Ulverston and District New Hospital Building Fund (1956) C.A.

The same principle applies even to the failure of charitable trusts, unless the funds are reapplied *cy-pres* (see Chapter 8). In this case, a fund was opened for a new hospital, but the scheme proved impracticable and there was a total failure. So far as money had been received from identifiable sources, there was a resulting trust in their favour. See also *Re British Red Cross Balkan Fund* (1914).

There has been much confusion in cases dealing with the dissolution of unincorporated associations. In most cases, the funds of such associations (both members' contributions and outside gifts) are held for the members subject to contractual rights and liabilities, and on dissolution such funds are to be divided among the existing members either in equal shares or as the rules of the association may otherwise determine (see *Re Sick and Funeral Society of St. John's Sunday School, Golcar*, 1972; and *Re Bucks Constabulary Widows and Orphans Fund Friendly Society (No. 2)*, 1978). Where, however, an association holds its funds on purpose or other trusts, and the association is dissolved or becomes redundant, such funds are held on resulting trusts for those who contributed them in shares relative to their contributions; *unless* the trusts are charitable and the funds can be re-applied *cy-pres*, or the court will (or may?) appoint a new trustee.

There are some situations where there will be no resulting trust, even though *prima facie* there should be one, because the donor parts with his money out and out without any intention of retaining any interest therein. Such a situation may indeed point to the fact that even "automatic resulting trusts" are in some sense dependent on the intentions of the donor. One can thus derelict an equitable interest, when as a last resort the property will go to the Crown as *bona vacantia*. This is probably the position in relation to money raised by means of street collections; and also perhaps by means of general entertainment, raffles and sweepstakes. See, generally, *Re West Sussex Constabulary's Widows Children and Benevolent (1930) Fund Trusts* (1970). *Cf. Re Gillingham Bus Disaster Fund*; Charities Act 1960 section 14.

7 Constructive Trusts

A good orthodox definition of constructive trusts is as follows: "Constructive trusts arise by operation of law. A constructive trust, in common will all other types of trust, is a relationship in respect of property under which one person, known as a trustee, is obliged to deal with property vested in him for the benefit of another person, known as a beneficiary. But, unlike all other trusts, a constructive trust is imposed by the court as a result of the conduct of the trustee and therefore arises quite independently of the intention of any of the parties." (*per* A. J. Oakley, *Constructive Trusts*, at p.l.).

The approach of the courts towards constructive trusts varies from the U.S.A. to England. American courts have imposed trusts whenever someone has been unjustly enriched at the expense of another — a trust is imposed primarily as a remedy to achieve justice between the parties. English courts have generally required more serious conduct to warrant imposing a trust, conduct amounting almost to a legal wrong in itself. Some recent decisions in the Court of Appeal, however, have raised suspicions that

English law is beginning to follow the American pattern. This shift of pattern has been widely criticised. Against the argument that the law should do its best to achieve justice as between the disputants in court, there are ranged the following points:

(i) The liability of a constructive trustee is considerable, and ought to be imposed only in the most obvious and worthy situations.

(ii) Constructive beneficiaries acquire equitable proprietary interests in the trust property, a factor which may cause difficulties in property rights and dealings, particularly where third parties are involved. In *Cooke* v. *Head* (1972), for example, the C.A., in order to do justice between a man and his mistress, imposed a constructive trust to vary the beneficial interests in the proceeds of sale of a bungalow which had been built by the man and his mistress. If the man had then become bankrupt, his creditors would have lost out to the mistress's right in the property, even though, say, they had provided the building materials. An equitable proprietary interest also gives one the standing for the powerful remedy of an equitable tracing claim. Further, imposing a constructive trust may divest a constructive trustee of his own beneficial interest. Property rights ought to be capable of certain definition, and not open to shifting in the light of fairness and reasonableness in all the circumstances. See remarks in *Pettitt* v. *Pettitt* (1970), *Gissing* v. *Gissing* (1971) and *Cowcher* v. *Cowcher* (1972).

A point which, it is suggested, needs much further discussion (but not here) is whether the "new model constructive trust," as Professor Pettit calls it, is really a substantive trust at all, or rather a mere remedy which does not necessarily carry with it all the incidents of the orthodox express trusts.

Two clear cases of constructive trusts are not dealt with here, because they are covered in land law courses. These are where a trust is imposed upon a vendor who has entered into a contract of sale which is capable of being specifically enforced; and where a trust is imposed upon a mortgagee.

1. Constructive trusts imposed because of fraudulent or unconscionable behaviour

The courts have always imposed trusts in the rare cases of fraudulent or unconscionable behaviour relating to *inter vivos* transactions. First, whenever there has been undue influence exercised, equity will intervene: *e.g.* where the relationship between parties to a transaction raises a presumption of undue influence; or where there is clear evidence of undue influence. The transaction can be set aside, and any property already transferred must be reconveyed. Secondly, no criminal may benefit from his crime. See *In the Estate of Crippen* (1911). Thirdly, a constructive trust is imposed where a person acquires property by fraudulent or unconscionable behaviour.

Bannister v. Bannister (1948) C.A.

D owned two adjacent cottages. D agreed with P orally during sale negotiations that D would continue to live in one of the cottages rent free for as long as she wished. The conveyance made no mention of the agreement. The C.A. imposed a constructive trust upon P to prevent his fraud, declaring that P held the cottage on trust to permit D to occupy it during her lifetime. It was, however, not made clear whether the life interest meant that D became a tenant for life under the Settled Land Act 1925, will all the ramifications this involves.

2. Constructive trusts imposed because of inequitable conduct

The courts are now beginning to impose trusts in situations where the behaviour of the constructive trustee is not fraudulent or unconscionable, but merely inequitable. Some of the criticisms of this approach have been outlined above. See also A. J. Oakley, *Constructive Trusts*, at pp. 19-21.

The earlier cases deal with the devolution of matrimonial property on the breakdown of marriage, now covered by section 25 Matrimonial Causes Act 1973. The principles enunciated still, however, cover cases of disputes arising during marriage, and, most importantly, disputes arising between persons not husband and wife.

Heseltine v. Heseltine (1971) C.A.

H and W had separated but not divorced. W had provided four-fifths of the purchase price of the matrimonial home, which was conveyed into H's name. W also advanced £40,000 to H, trusting in his advice that this would avoid estate duty if she predeceased him. W also transferred £20,000 to H to assist him in becoming a "name" at Lloyd's. During the marriage, four houses had been purchased out of W's funds, and transferred into H's name. The C.A. disregarded the certainty of the law of resulting trusts, and imposed a constructive trust. The matrimonial house was held three-quarters to W, one-quarter to H; and the rest of the property on trust for W (disregarding the fact that W must have intended from the very terms of the gifts that H keep the £40,000 and £20,000 beneficially).

Cooke v. Head (1972) C.A.

P was D's mistress. P and D decided to build a bungalow. D paid all the outgoings. P helped greatly in the physical work of building the bungalow. P, on the break-up, claimed a share in the proceeds of sale of the bungalow. The C.A. imposed a constructive trust, on the grounds that the two parties had by their joint efforts acquired the property to be used for their joint benefit. See also *Eves* v. *Eves* (1975), but *cf.* approach of Browne L.J. and Brightman J. in that case.

Hussey v. Palmer (1972) C.A.

P was asked by her son-in-law and daughter to live with them. Because the house was small, P paid for an extension to be added. Differences developed, and P left. P claimed repayment of the money spent on the extension under a resulting trust. The C.A. held she was entitled to the money because there was a constructive trust. This gave her an equitable interest in the house proportionate to the relative expenditure of the parties.

Binions v. Evans (1972) C.A.

The Tredegar Estate entered into an agreement with D that she could live rent free in one of their cottages for the rest of her life, if she kept it in good repair. P bought the cottage, at a lower than market price because it was expressly subject to D's right to reside there. P subsequently claimed possession from D. Two judges imposed a constructive trust on the authority of *Bannister* v. *Bannister*. Lord Denning M.R. held that D was a contractual licensee, but, instead of granting her an injunction to prevent P from evicting her, he held she could enforce her license by imposing a constructive trust, which would provide a just and equitable solution.

See also *DHN Food Distributors* v. *London Borough of Tower Hamlets* (1976).

3. *Constructive trusts imposed as a result of a breach of fiduciary duty*

Constructive trusts are imposed wherever a fiduciary has obtained a benefit as a result of a breach of the duty of loyalty which he owes to his principal. Fiduciary obligations arise as between trustee and beneficiary, agent and principal, director and company, and partner and co-partner, and in some instances in relation to solicitors, accountants, etc. The quality of the fiduciary obligation tends to vary with the relationship, but the general attitude of English law to fiduciaries is a harsh one.

(a) Purchase of property by a fiduciary from his principal

A sale of property to a trustee from his trust must be set

aside, see *Ex p. Lacey* (1802). The honesty of the trustee, the openness of the transaction, and the fairness of price are not material; see *Wright* v. *Morgan* (1926).

Cf. Holder v. Holder (1968) C.A.

An executor of a will renounced his executorship after he had intermeddled with the estate. He was tenant of some farms which the other executors offered for sale subject to his tenancy. He himself purchased the farm at auction for a good price, well above the reserve. The C.A. refused to set aside the sales, two judges saying that the matter was one for the discretion of the court exercisable after the relevant knowledge and intentions of the parties had been ascertained.

As a result of this factual approach, it may be that purchases of trust property by trustees will not automatically be set aside. This has always been the position in purchases of property by other types of fiduciaries from their principals. A trust may be imposed where a sale is set aside, and the fiduciary already has the property or has resold it.

(b) Purchase by a fiduciary of the beneficial interest of his principal

Such purchases are upheld if the fiduciary can show that he has obtained no advantage as a result of his position as fiduciary.

(c) Sale by a fiduciary of his own property to his principal

The sale will be set aside, disregarding the honesty and fairness of the fiduciary, unless he has fully disclosed his interest in the transaction.

Bentley v. Craven (1853)

D was responsible for purchasing sugar for a partnership of refiners of which he was a member. He also had an independent business as a dealer. He bought sugar which he resold to the partnership at a profit, although at market price. He was held liable to account for the profit to the partnership.

(d) Competition by a fiduciary with the business of the principal

A partner may not compete (s.30 Partnership Act 1890); a trustee may not set up in competition (see *Re Thomson*, 1930); a director is probably under a duty not to compete with his company. An injunction may be brought to restrain any competition, and a fiduciary may have to account for any profit made as a result of the competition.

(e) Remuneration obtained by a fiduciary as a result of his position.

A trustee must generally act without payment, unless payment is authorised by the trust instrument, agreement with the beneficiaries, or by the court (s.42 Trustee Act 1925). Further, if a trustee by virtue of that trusteeship holds an office of profit, he must account to the trust for any remuneration he receives from that office; see *Re Macadam* (1946); unless he is in some way authorised or obtains remuneration really because of his own standing, rather than *qua* trustee.

These harsh rules do not apply to other fiduciaries.

Where a trustee has to account for remuneration, a constructive trust may be imposed if the property is identifiable; or there may be only an action for damages.

(f) Speculation by a fiduciary with the property of his principal

A principal in this case is entitled to all profits made by the fiduciary, under a constructive trust.

(g) Use by a fiduciary of confidential information obtained by virtue of his fiduciary position

Boardman v. Phipps (1967) H.L.

A trust solicitor was concerned about the investments of

a trust fund. He suggested the acquisition of a majority holding in a particular company, but the trustees said this was out of the question. With a beneficiary, the solicitor went ahead and purchased shares in the company for themselves. The move resulted in a profit of £47,000 for the trust, and £75,000 for the beneficiary and solicitor. In the take-over negotiations the solicitor had obtained information by virtue of his position as solicitor to the trust. The H.L. upheld a claim by the trust fund for the profit of £75,000, on the basis of a constructive trust imposed for use of confidential information to gain a profit.

The decision has been criticised, and it has been suggested that a constructive trust should only be imposed where, after a full examination of the facts, it is clear that the fiduciary placed himself in a position where there was a serious possibility of conflict between his own interest and his duty. Such an approach is evident in *Seager* v. *Copydex* (1967).

Cf. **Industrial Development Consultants v. Cooley (1972) Ch. Div.**

D was managing director of P Co. During unsuccessful negotiations for a design contract, on behalf of P Co., from the Eastern Gas Board, it was intimated to D that he could expect to be awarded the contract if he acted independently. D thus lied to the company and secured a release from his contract. P Co.'s claim that D was a trustee of the contract he later obtained from the Gas Board, and therefore liable to account for his profits, succeeded.

(h) **Transactions by a fiduciary with a third party in breach of his fiduciary duty**

A trustee who abuses his position by entering into a transaction with a third party must account for the benefit of the transaction as constructive trustee. See *Keech* v. *Sandford* (1726). This is a harsh rule and has been applied to a range of fiduciary relationships and transactions.

(i) Other secret profits obtained by a fiduciary out of his fiduciary position

In all cases of secret profits, other than bribe, a fiduciary will be constructive trustee of that profit. See *Williams* v. *Barton* (1927); *Reading* v. *Attorney-General* (1951). *Lister and Co.* v. *Stubbs* (1980) suggests that where the profit is a bribe, the relationship which arises is one of debtor-creditor rather than of trustee-beneficiary.

4. *Constructive trusts imposed upon a stranger who has dealt with or received property which has reached his hands as a result of a breach of a fiduciary duty*

In certain situations, a constructive trust will be imposed upon the stranger, if there is identifiable property in his hands. Other remedies may also be available against the transferor. There are several classes of transferee.

(a) Bona fide purchasers for value of a legal estate in the property without notice of a trust

They cannot be constructive trustees; and therefore take free.

(b) Innocent volunteers

A tracing claim exists for the beneficiary, but an innocent volunteer will not be a constructive trustee. See *Re Diplock* (1948). It is probable that before a tracing claim can be brought, the beneficiary must exhaust all other remedies he has; thus, an innocent volunteer is liable only to the extent that the transferors cannot compensate the beneficiaries for their loss.

(c) Intermeddlers in the administration of a trust, or trustees de son tort

Any trustee de son tort is a constructive trustee of any property acquired by him in the course of his intermeddling; see *Lyell* v. *Kennedy* (1889).

(d) Transferees with notice of a trust

Such transferee, whether or not he has given consideration, is bound by that trust. Therefore, he holds the property transferred to him as a constructive trustee.

The notice required is actual, or constructive (where the transferee ought to have known of the trust).

Nelson v. Larholt (1948) K.B. Div.

An executor of a will drew eight cheques on the estate's bank account, all signed by him as executor, in favour of D, who cashed the cheques in good faith. Denning J. held that D must be taken to have known what any reasonable man would have known, that the executor was in breach of trust. Therefore, D was a constructive trustee of the property.

(e) Agents

In *Barnes* v. *Addy* (1874) Lord Selbourne L.C. laid down the principle that constructive trusts will not be imposed upon agents acting honestly in the course of their agency. This is the only sensible approach to take to facilitate the undertaking of normal business transactions. Any agent who misconducts himself by acting in excess of his authority becomes a constructive trustee of any property in his hands. Any agent who honestly follows the instructions of his principal will not be liable as a constructive trustee, even if the principal is acting in breach of his fiduciary obligation.

Williams-Ashman v. Price and Williams (1942) Ch. Div.

Trust solicitors, following instructions from the trustee, paid out trust moneys to persons not beneficiaries, and invested the residue in unauthorised investments. The solicitors had in their possession a copy of the trust instrument, and could have checked in. It was held that there could be no constructive trust on the solicitors because they had acted honestly in the course of their agency without *actual* notice of any breach of trust.

In *Selangor United Rubber Estates* v. *Cradock (no. 3)* (1968) Ungoed-Thomas J. imposed a constructive trust on a bank on the grounds of their *constructive* notice of a breach of trust — the bank had clearly acted in good faith without any knowledge of the breach of trust, but a reasonable banker would in the circumstances, have realised that a breach of trust was being perpetrated. This approach was adopted in *Karak Rubber Co.* v. *Burden (No. 2)* (1972), but doubted in favour of the traditional view in *Carl-Zeiss Stiftung* v. *Herbert Smith (No. 2)* (1969), *Competitive Insurance Co.* v. *Davies Investments* (1975), and *Belmont Finance Corporation* v. *Williams Furniture* (1977). The traditional view is generally preferred.

[It is further suggested "that a transferee of trust property who innocently but negligently fails to make the enquiries which a reasonable man would have made should clearly be bound by a trust but should not be held liable as a constructive trustee." *per* A. J. Oakley, *Constructive Trusts*, at pp. 72-73. Oakley's suggestion disposes of the inconsistency in result which otherwise exists between cases of agents with *constructive* notice and cases of transferees with *constructive* notice (*cf. Nelson* v. *Larholt*).]

8 Charity—Definition, Schemes and *Cy-pres*

"Charitable purposes are those which are considered to be of such value and importance to the community that they receive especially favourable treatment." (*per* Hanbury and Maudsley, *Modern Equity*, 10th edit., at p. 367). Such

purposes were summarised by Lord Macnaghten in
Commissioners of Special Income Tax v. *Pemsel* (1891) as
being the relief of poverty, the advancement of education,
and of religion, and other purposes beneficial to the
community. The original "definition" of charitable purposes
is found in the Preamble to the Charitable Uses Act 1601,
and since 1601 purposes within the spirit and intendment,
or within the equity, of the statute have been regarded as
legally charitable. The matter of definition is governed by
the case law, and the decisions of the Charity Commissioners
on the issue of registration of charities under section 4
Charities Act 1960.

Charitable, or public purpose trusts, enjoy considerable
advantages:

(a) The human beneficiary principle does not operate so
as to invalidate them, because they are public
trusts enforceable by the Attorney-General;
although general administration is carried out by
the Charity Commissioners.

(b) No test of certainty of a particular form of purpose
applies. A gift on trust for charitable purposes is
valid. The court and the Charity Commissioners
can establish a sheme to cover the detailed
application of the funds. The only test of
certainty applicable is that the gift must be for
purposes exclusively charitable.

(c) Charitable trusts may be of perpetual duration.
However, the rule against perpetuities governs the
remoteness of vesting in the case of gifts to
charities in the same way as it governs remoteness
in the case of other gifts. For gifts coming into
effect after July 15, 1964 the wait and see
provision of the Perpetuities and Accumulations
Act 1964 apply. See, generally, land law courses.
The rule in *Christ's Hospital* v. *Grainger* (1849)
provides an exception, in that a gift over *from
one charity to another charity* is valid even if it
takes effect outside the perpetuity period, because

the original vesting is deemed as one *for charitable purposes* in general.

(d) Charitable trusts enjoy enormous fiscal advantages in the form of various exemptions.

1. *The definition of charitable purposes — The element of benefit*

Lord Macnaghten's classification is not a precise definition, but provides a convenient summary. Each head of the classification involves two separate elements — the element of *benefit*, inherent in relief of poverty, and advancement of education and religion, but to be ascertained specifically in cases under the general head "beneficial to the community;" and the element of *public* benefit, the purpose benefitting the whole community or a substantial section of it.

(a) The relief of poverty

Poverty is a matter of degree; it is not destitution, but perhaps "going short." It covers gifts for the poor, the needy and the indigent, even when limited to particular locations or religions or groupings. Gifts for persons of limited means, gentlewomen or distressed gentlefolk are included. There needs to be a qualification of poverty. See, generally, *Re Coulthurst's Will Trusts* (1951); *Re Lewis* (1955); and *Re Cohen* (1973). A gift may be charitable even if for immediate capital distribution, rather than an endowment; and the trustees are permitted a discretion in choosing which among a class are to benefit.

The relief of poverty is adequate; the element of *public* benefit does not operate in this area.

Re Scarisbrick (1951) C.A.

A trust was upheld "for such relations of my . . . son and daughters as in the opinion of the survivor of my . . . son and daughters shall be in needy circumstances . . . as the survivor . . . shall by deed or will appoint."

This approach was followed by the House of Lords in *Dingle* v. *Turner* (1972) in a "poor employees" rather than "poor relations" gift.

There will be no charitable trust, however, even in a poverty case, where the persons to be benefitted are actually *specified* individuals. This is a private trust, because the gift is merely to particular poor people, the relief of poverty among them being no more than the motive of the gift.

(b) The advancement of education

The concept of educational charity now covers "almost any form of worthwhile instruction or cultural advancement, except for purely professional or career courses." (*per* Hanbury and Maudsley, *Modern Equity*, 10th edit., at p. 378). Examples abound: the founding of lectureships; the promotion of music, art and drama; the establishment of museums and cultural societies; the production of a dictionary; the publication of Law Reports; etc. Education is more than knowledge — it involves teaching and the dissemination of knowledge. Research, to be charitable, must improve the sum of communicable knowledge. See *Re Shaw* (1957), *Re Hopkins* (1965). Artistic and aesthetic education may be charitable. See *Re Delius* (1957). The determination of the educational value of a gift rests upon an evaluation of its quality and usefulness. Sometimes expert evidence may prove helpful.

Re Pinion (1965) C.A.

A testator give his studio, with its contents, to trustees for the establishment of a museum of his collection of furniture and objets d'art, and paintings. Expert opinion was offered that the collection had little artistic merit. The trust was held void, Harman J. referring to "the mass of junk."

Gifts for sports which are an essential part of schooling or other education are charitable.

Re Mariette (1915) Ch. Div.

A gift to provide, *inter alia*, Eton fives courts and squash rackets courts at Aldenham School was upheld because games were an inherent part of a public school education.

Cf. I.R.C. v. McMullen (1978) C.A.

A trust for the promotion of the playing of games and sports by pupils of schools and universities generally was held not to be charitable as there was no clear link between the playing of games and the education of the pupils as a whole.

Professional bodies may be charitable if they exist for educational purposes; *e.g.* Royal College of Surgeons, Royal College of Nursing, Construction Industry Training Board. Gifts which are really for political purposes, but couched in educational terms, will not be charitable.

Cf. Re Snowcroft (1898) Ch. Div.

A gift "for the furtherance of Conservative principles and religions and mental improvement" was upheld. See also *Re Bushnell* (1975).

(c) The advancement of religion

Religion is difficult to define, but Lord Parker in *Bowman v. Secular Society* (1917) referred to any form of monotheistic theism as being a religion. A gift to be charitable must *advance* religion — "the promotion of spiritual teaching in a wide sense, and the maintenance of the doctrines on which this rests, and the observances that serve to promote and manifest it — not merely a foundation or cause to which it can be related" — (see *Karen Kayemeth Le Jisroel v. I.R.C.*, 1931). No distinction is drawn between the Established Church and other Christian sects, and sometimes very questionable gifts are upheld as charitable (see *Re Watson*, 1973; *Thornton v. Howe*, 1862). It seems that non-Christian religions will be accorded charitable status.

Some purposes are charitable as being religious, but do not advance spiritual teaching; *e.g.* erection of churches and maintenance of such buildings; benefitting the clergy or choir; "for God's work in the parish;" etc.

(d) Other purposes beneficial to the community

When are gifts for other purposes beneficial in a legally charitable manner? A purpose mentioned specifically in the Preamble is charitable; so is a purpose already upheld as charitable in a previous case. However, not every public purpose is legally rather than factually beneficial — it is only if it is beneficial within the spirit and intendment or the equity of the Preamble, or can be argued to be beneficial on analogy with decided cases, that is becomes legally charitable.

Williams' Trustees v. I.R.C. (1947) H.L.

A trust for promoting the interests of the Welsh community in London failed. Lord Simonds stated:
" . . . every object of public general utility is not necessarily a charity."

Cf. Scottigh Burial Reform and Cremation Society Ltd. v. Glasgow Corporation (1968) H.L.

A non-profit making cremation society was upheld as charitable, by analogy with cases taking the "repair of churches" to the maintenance of burial grounds in church-yards, and then to burial in graveyards beyond churchyards. It was a natural progression to cremation.

The obligation of the Charity Commissioners to register Charities (imposed under Charities Act 1960) has led to the emergence of a wide range of "precedent" under the fourth general head.

More importantly, however, it is suggested that recent pronouncements indicate that the courts are beginning to articulate a general principle which will come to be the primary tool in assessing the charitability of a gift, with analogy to the Preamble and decided cases becoming a secondary tool only. A suggested version of this principle (from myself) is as follows: "A purpose is charitable if it is one on which public funds are at present being spent, or would properly be spent if there were adequate public funds to go around." Is such a principle workable? The fact that the courts or Charity Commissioners would still need to determine those purposes on which public money *ought* to be spent gives the courts a wide (some argue too subjective) discretion, which may be undesirable. However, unless one provides a (statutory?) list of purposes, which itself would suffer from gross inflexibility, the courts will always be needed to exercise a discretion in this area. See most clearly *National Anti-Vivisection Society* v. *I.R.C.* (1948). The principle suggested provides for a simplification and rationalisation of the manner in which the courts exercise their discretion.

Is there any support for such a principle?

(i) The Recreational Charities Act 1958 refers to the interests of social welfare as a test to be satisfied in determining the charitability of provision of facilities for recreation or other leisure-time occupation.

(ii) In the *Scottish Cremation Case*, Lord Wilberforce said: "The group 'repair of bridges, ports, havens, causeways, churches, sea banks and highways' has within it the common element of public utility and it is of interest to note that the original label of Lord Macnaghten's fourth category 'other purposes beneficial to the community' affixed by Sir Samuel Romilly in *Morice* v. *Bishop of Durham* was ' . . . the advancement of objects of general public utility.' In this context I find it of significance that Parliament in 1902 by the Cremation Act of that year placed cremation, as a public service, on the same footing as burial."

(iii) In *Incorporated Council of Law Reporting* v. *Attorney-General* (1971) Russell L.J. suggested that if a purpose is *prima facie* beneficial to the community, then it is *prima facie* charitable unless it is shown to be otherwise. He went on: "If I look at the somewhat random examples in the preamble to the statute I find in the repair of bridges, havens, causeways, sea banks and highways examples of matters which if not looked after by private enterprise must be a proper function and responsibility of government, which would afford strong ground for a statutory expression by Parliament of anxiety to prevent misappropriation of funds voluntarily dedicated to such matters. It cannot I think be doubted that if there were not a competent and reliable set of reports of judicial decisions, it would be a proper function and responsibility of government to secure their provision for the due administration of the law."

It should be noted that the suggested principle is wide enough to encompass within it the relief of poverty and the advancement of education. The advancement of religion would, it is suggested, become the only anomalous case of charity.

Examples of gifts upheld under the fourth head: trusts for the relief of the aged, impotent and sick; trusts for social, recreational or sporting facilities (see Recreational Charities Act, 1958; *cf. I.R.C.* v. *Baddeley*, 1955); trusts for the welfare of animals. Trusts for political purposes are not charitable — see *Re Bushnell* (1975); *Bowman* v. *Secular Society* (1917); *National Anti-Vivisection Society* v. *I.R.C.* (1948).

2. *The definition of charitable purposes — The benefit must be public*

(a) **Poverty Cases**
See previous discussion.

(b) Education

A charitable trust must be for the benefit of the community or an appreciably important class of the community, a class which is not numerically negligible. "A trust for the advancement of education is charitable if it is for the education of the public or of a section of the public which is not selected on the basis of *a personal nexus or connection*, either with the donor or between themselves." (*per* Hanbury and Maudsley, *op. cit.*, at p. 401).

Oppenheim v. Tobacco Securities Trust Co. (1951) H.L.

Income was to be applied in "providing for . . . the education of children of employees or former employees of the British-American Tobacco Company Ltd. . . . or any of its subsidiary or allied companies in such manner . . . as the acting trustees shall in their absolute discretion . . . think fit;" and there was power to use capital also. The number of employees eligible exceeded 100,000. It was held that there was a personal nexus between members of the class of beneficiaries, and they did not constitute a section of the public.

The *Oppenheim* reasoning was criticised in *Dingle* v. *Turner*, and all five Law Lords agreed with Lord McDermott (who dissented in *Oppenheim*) that in each case it was a matter of degree depending upon the particular facts. The *Oppenheim* test was not overruled, however, as *Dingle* v. *Turner* was a "poor employees" case, and not subject to a *public* benefit requirement.

(c) Religion

A trust will be charitable if it offers advancement of a religious activity to the public or a section of the public — the *actual* number who participate is not relevant. A cloistered, enclosed or monastic activity is not charitable; see *Gilmour* v. *Coats* (1949). It is established that the saying of prayers without more is not for the public benefit (*cf. Re Caus*, 1934).

Neville Estates Ltd. v. Madden (1962) Ch. Div.
A trust for the advancement of religion among the members of Catford synagogue was upheld as charitable. Some benefit would accrue to the public because those attending the synagogue would mix with others outside.

It may be that in religion cases there must be some element of benefit to the public as a whole, rather than that the participants themselves should benefit.

(d) Other purposes

Benefits which are generally available, although only taken up by a few, are charitable. A limitation to a geographical locality does not matter; but a limitation by personal nexus invalidates the gift. The persons to be benefitted must be the whole community, or *all* the inhabitants of a particular area. A class within a class will not do, *e.g.* "Welsh people in London." Lord Cross in *Dingle* v. *Turner* suggested a more flexible approach: it "is a question of degree and cannot be by itself decisive of the question whether the trust is a charity. Much must depend on the purpose of the trust. It may well be that, on the one hand, a trust to promote some purpose, *prima facie* charitable, will constitute a charity even though the class of potential beneficiaries might fairly be called a private class and that, on the other hand, a trust to promote another purpose, also *prima facie* charitable, will not constitute a charity even though the class of potential beneficiaries might seem to some people fairly describable as a section of the public."

3. *The purposes must be exclusively charitable*

The main purpose of the trust must be charitable. *Subsidiary* non-charitable purposes will not invalidate the trust.

I.R.C. v. City of Glasgow Police Athletic Association (1953) H.L.

A police athletic association, intended to benefit policemen in Glasgow was not wholly ancillary to increasing the efficiency of the Glasgow police force and therefore not charitable.

Re Cole (1958) C.A.

A gift was on trust "for the general benefit and general welfare of the children for the time being" of a council maintained home for children. The home was charitable, but the gift failed, because its terms were wide enough to permit trustees to spend money on non-charitable purposes, such as the provision of TV sets.

The *and/or* cases present a strange picture. If a gift is for "charitable *and* philanthropic purposes" it will be valid, because the purposes must be both at the same time. If a gift is for "charitable *or* philanthropic purposes" it fails, since philanthropy is wider than charity.

It is sometimes possible to sever the failed portion of a total gift from that which is good, thus allowing the latter to go through. See *Salusbury* v. *Denton* (1857).

4. *The doctrine of cy-pres*

In some cases where property is given for charitable purposes and the purposes cannot be carried out in the precise manner intended by the donor, the cy-pres doctrine enables the court (or Charity Commissioners) to make a scheme for the application of the property for other charitable purposes as near as possible to those intended by the donor. (Where there is a gift to charity but not upon trust, it can be disposed of by the Crown.)

A distinction exists between cases of initial failure — where there is a possibility of the property being held on resulting trust unless cy-pres operates — and cases of subsequent failure — where the property has already been applied to charity and there is no resulting trust, without an express provision of a gift over to take effect within the perpetuity period.

(a) Subsequent failure

Re Wright (1954) C.A.

A testatrix who died in 1933 provided for the foundation, on the death of a tenant for life, of a convalescent home for impecunious gentlewomen. It was a practicable scheme in 1933, but probably not in 1942 when the tenant for life died. The C.A. held that dedication of the property to charity had occurred in 1933. The possibility of lapse or resulting trust was excluded, there being no express provision to the contrary. Cy-pres was thus ordered.

See also *Re King* (1923); but *cf. Re Stanford* (1924).

(b) Initial failure

A charitable trust which fails at the date of the gift will either fail and fall into residue, or the property will be applied cy-pres. The width of the charitable intention manifested by the donor is the vital factor.

Where the intention is that the property be applied for a specific purpose which fails, or for a specific charitable institution which disappears, the gift will fail.

Re Rymer (1895) C.A.

A legacy was left "to the rector for the time being of St. Thomas' Seminary for the education of priests for the diocese of Westminster." By the testator's death the Seminary had closed down, and the students had gone elsewhere. The gift failed, because the C.A. construed it as one "to a particular seminary for the purposes thereof."

Where the gift is to an institution which has never existed, it may be easier to construe the intention of the donor to give to charitable purposes in general. See *Re Harwood* (1936) and *Re Spence* (1978).

Where there exists a wider intention — called a paramount or general charitable intention — the property will be applied cy-pres. The matter is essentially one of construction.

In some cases it is possible to identify a successor of the now defunct named charity, or at the very least to identify the recipient of that charity's funds on its dissolution. The property will be applied in favour of the successor.

Courts are liberal in determining which institutions are intended, and mere slips of the pen are disregarded. See *Re Faraker* (1912).

Where a gift is for a purpose rather than to an institution, the question is whether that purpose is on the balance of probabilities capable or incapable of fulfilment. If incapable, the gift will fail and fall into residue, unless it is saved for cy-pres application by a wider charitable intent. The matter is again one of construction.

(c) Charities Act 1960

The Act has had no effect on the law relating to initial failure (except under s.14). It is still necessary to decide on the question of impossibility or impracticability of performance at the time of the gift, whether it be a gift for a purpose or for an institution.

Section 13 provides for the application of cy-pres in five far-reaching circumstances of impossibility or impracticability (see s.13(1)) where the width of charitable intention has no operation (see s.13(2)). The application of cy-pres is mandatory and, therefore, the trustees are under a duty to have the relevant property applied cy-pres.

Section 14 provides for application cy-pres, regardless of width of intent or of initial or subsequent failure, where money has been paid by a donor who cannot be identified or found, or who has signed a disclaimer. The proceeds of collecting boxes, lotteries and similar fund raising activities are deemed to belong to donors who cannot be identified.

Index

Advancement,
  presumption of, 59-62
Animals, trust for, 16
Attorney-General, 2, 12

Cestui Que trust,
  See, Express trust
Charitable trust, 76-84
  non-charitable purpose
    trust compared with, 12
    perpetual duration, of, 76
    poverty, for relief of, 77
    public benefit, require-
      ment of, 12, 77, 82
    public or sector of the
      public, for, 83
    religion, for advance-
      ment of, 79, 83
    scheme for application
      of, 76
  classification, of, 76
  cy-pres doctrine,
    definition, 75, 76
Classification,
  private trusts and public
    (charitable) trusts, 11
  trust, of, 2
Consideration,
  beneficiary, provision by, 33
  marriage, 33
Constructive trusts,
  breach of fiduciary duty,
    because of, 69
  definition, of, 65
  fraudulent or uncon-
    scionable behaviour,
    because of, 67
    undue influence, 67
  inequitable conduct, because
    of, 67
    husband and wife, of, 68
    persons not husband and
      wife, of, 68

new model, 66
stranger receiving trust
  property, 73
tracing, 73
unjust enrichment, 65
Contract,
  trust, to create, 34
Cy-pres doctrine,
  circumstances where
    applicable, 85
  general charitable inten-
    tion, 86, 87
  impossibility or impractica-
    bility, 87
  modification of rule, 85-87
  scheme for application of
    property of charitable
    trust, 85

Discretionary trust,
  certainty test, 8
  trust power, mere power,
    distinguished, 7

Equitable interest,
  contract to assign, 22
  contract to dispose of, 21
  disposition of, 24-27
    stamp duty on, attempts
      to avoid, 27
  will, disposition by, 22
Equity,
  acts in personam, 12
  corruption, turns its face
    against, 40
  trust, creation of, 1
  vain, in, will do nothing, 40
  volunteer, will not assist, 33,
    40
    exceptions, 43
Express trust,
  animals, for maintenance
    or benefit of, 16

bare trust, 2
certainty, prerequisite, of,
    3-10
    certainty of actual bene-
        fit interests, 5
    certainty of bene-
        ficiaries/objects, 5, 9,
        10
    certainty of subject-
        matter, 4, 5
    certainty of words or
        intention, 3
cestui que trust, require-
    ment of, 14
    volunteer, as, 29
complete constitution,
    prerequisite, of, 29-43
    declaration of self as
        trustee, where, 29
    declaration of trust by
        transfer, where, 30-33
    trust of the promise,
        where, 36
    unenforceable contract,
        where based upon,
        41-43
contract to create, 21, 34
    intending settlor and
        intended trustee,
        between, 38-41
    land, 21
    personalty, 22
    settlor and intended bene-
        ficiary, between, 34
declaration, of, 22-28
    declaration of self as
        trustee, by, 22
    declaration of trust by
        transfer, 23
    inter vivos, 22, *et seq.*
    land, 23
    meaning, 22
    personalty, 24
    sub-trust, nature of, 22,
        23
    disposition, as, 24-27
discretionary trust, 2,
    And see, Discretionary
    trust
fixed trust, 2
    certainty of benefici-
        aries/objects test, 6

formalities, prerequisite, of,
    21-28
human beneficiary, pre-
    requisite, of, 10-20
imperative nature of trust, 6
masses, for saying of, 16
monument or grave, for
    erection or maintenance,
    of, 16
non-charitable purpose trust,
    11-20
    certainty of objects, 15
    certainty of purposes, 15
    enforceability of, 12-14
    perpetuities, rule against,
        application to, 17
    unincorporated associa-
        tions, 18
precatory words, effect of, 3
power distinguished, 5
    certainty, requirements
        of, 8
resulting trust, on failure of,
    5, 6, 10, 46
Secret trust,
    See, Secret trusts
unincorporated associa-
    tions, for benefit of,
    16-19
    joint tenants or tenants
        in common, members
        as, 19
will, creation by, 22

Fraud,
    statute not to be used as
        instrument of, 28

Implied trust,
    See Resulting trust

Part performance,
    doctrine of, 28
        constructive trust,
            replaced by, 28
Perpetuities, rule against,
    charitable trust, application
        to, 76
    non-charitable purpose
        trusts, application to, 17
Power,
    discretionary nature of, 6

mere power of appointment,
6, 7
trust compared with, 5
certainty, differing re-
quirements of, 8
trust implied in default of
appointment, 7
trust power, 7
discretionary trust,
distinguished, 7
Precatory words,
effect of, 3
Resulting trust,
beneficial interest, failure to
exhaust, 54, 62
charitable trust, on failure
of, 64
classification, of, 55
automatic resulting trust,
54
presumed resulting trust,
54
deposit at banks in joint
names, 59
displaced by presumption of
advancement, 56, 59,
And see, Advancement
failure of express trust, on,
5, 6, 10
husband and wife, application to, 56
marriage settlement, under,
where no marriage, 63
money raised by collections,
etc., 65
bona vacantia, as, 65
money raised by subscrip-
tion, 63
purchase in name of another,
54
rebuttal of presumption, of,
56

voluntary conveyance into
name of another, 54
land, of, 56
personality, of, 56, 57
unincorporated associations,
on dissolution of, 64
will, under, 63

Secret trusts,
enforcement of, justification for, 44-47
express or constructive,
whether, 49, 50
fully secret trust, 44, 50, 51
requirements, of, 50-52
sealed envelope, details
handed over in, 51
tenants in common or
joint tenants, gifts to,
51
half-secret trust, 44, 52
requirements, of, 52, 53
inter vivos gifts, application
to, 50
operate outside will, 47-49
secret trustee predeceasing
testator, 48
Statute,
fraud, not to be used as
instrument of, 28, 45,
et seq.

Taxation,
establishment of trust to
avoid, 1
Trustee,
obligation to account, 71
payment, duty to act
without, 71

Unit trust, 2